HOW TO
MAKE A
MILLION
BEFORE LUNCH

Rachel Bridge is the Enterprise Editor at *The Sunday Times* where she writes about entrepreneurs and small business. She has written three books about entrepreneurs: *How I Made It*, *My Big Idea* and *You Can Do It Too*. She has an MA in Economics from Cambridge University.

HOW TO MAKE A MILLION BEFORE LUNCH

Rachel Bridge

First published in 2010 by Virgin Books, an imprint of Ebury Publishing
A Random House Group Company

This edition published in 2011 by Virgin Books

2 4 6 8 10 9 7 5 3 1

Every reasonable effort has been made to contact the copyright holders of material reproduced in this book. If any have inadvertently been overlooked, the publishers would be glad to hear from them and make good in future editions any errors or omissions brought to their attention.

Some of the material reproduced in this book was first published in *The Sunday Times*.

www.eburypublishing.co.uk

www.randomhouse.co.uk

Address for companies within The Random House Group Limited can be found at
www.randomhouse.co.uk/offices.htm

The Random House Group Limited Reg. No. 954009

A CIP catalogue record for this book is available from the British Library

ISBN 9780753539576

The Random House Group Limited supports The Forest Stewardship Council (FSC®), the leading international forest certification organisation. Our books carrying the FSC label are printed on FSC® certified paper. FSC is the only forest certification scheme endorsed by the leading environmental organisations, including Greenpeace. Our paper procurement policy can be found at www.randomhouse.co.uk/environment

Typeset by Palimpsest Book Production Limited, Falkirk, Stirlingshire
Printed in the UK by CPI Bookmarque, Croydon, CR0 4TD

For Harry and Jack

CONTENTS

ACKNOWLEDGEMENTS

It has been an amazing experience writing this book and there are lots of people who have been a real source of help and inspiration to me along the way. I would really like to thank all the entrepreneurs mentioned in this book for their time and generosity in sharing their experiences. I would also like to thank all the entrepreneurs and small business owners I have met at conferences and events around the country over the past few years for taking the time to share their thoughts with me.

An enormous thank you to my agent Pat Lomax and to Ed Faulkner and everyone at Virgin Books for being brilliant in every way.

Thank you to *The Sunday Times*, especially Editor John Witherow, Business Editor Dominic O'Connell and Managing Editor Richard Caseby. Thank you also to Kathleen Herron for her constant and unfailing encouragement in everything I do.

Finally, I would like to thank my family and friends for their support and good advice. Sarah, Toby and Ronnie – I couldn't have done it without you. And a big hug to Harry and Jack, just for being there and making everything wonderful.

Rachel Bridge
London

INTRODUCTION

These days almost everyone wants to become an entrepreneur and start up a business of their own. It is not hard to see why. The prospect of being your own boss and taking control of your own destiny – and perhaps ultimately ending up with a huge sum of money – is extremely alluring.

The one thing that deters people from taking the plunge and doing it themselves is that setting up a business from scratch – and actually managing to make money from it – seems to take such a long time and require so much effort, money and energy.

By the time you've researched your idea and applied for a huge bank loan, then kitted out an office and opened a shop, and employed some people and then moved to bigger offices and opened another shop, and applied for an even bigger loan, it seems it's going to be for ever before you finally get to sail off into the sunset waving a fat cheque.

The good news is that there is another way of doing it and this book will tell you how. I am going to show you the short cuts to success; how to cut out all the unnecessary stuff you don't need to do; and how to focus on the important things you really do need to do in order to turn your business idea into a thriving reality. I can't promise that you will make your first million before lunch, but if you follow the short cuts in this book then I can promise to get you there a whole lot quicker.

Thinking of inventing a product from scratch? Or opening a shop on the high street? Or employing a team of staff? Well, don't. All these classic start-up approaches are time-wasting, money-draining, energy-sapping diversions. They will merely bog you down in red tape and paperwork. They will not only hold you back, they could seriously damage your chances of success.

This book will show you how to cut out all the time-wasting stuff from every stage of the entrepreneur journey; from having the idea in the first place, to thinking about how to structure it, to launching the business and then growing it. And finally, of course, to selling it, the point at which our journey both begins and ends.

Along the way I will tell you what sort of businesses you should be starting up – and what kind of enterprises you should avoid at all costs.

Some of my suggestions are fairly radical, others are basic common sense. Some reflect the fast-changing world we live in, others are central tenets for all successful businesses.

But the best bit is, they actually work.

As the Enterprise Editor of *The Sunday Times* and the author of several books about entrepreneurs, I've spent many years watching successful entrepreneurs in action and talking to them about how they achieved their success – about the things they wish they had done, and the things they wish they hadn't. I've also talked to the entrepreneurs who failed, and found out what tripped them up.

The fact is that as a first-time entrepreneur you can waste huge amounts of time, energy and money on unnecessary things, simply because you don't know a better way of going about it. And that is not just frustrating, it is potentially fatal for your business. In the early days of running a business you simply don't have the luxury of being able to make expensive, time-consuming mistakes. The commercial world is not a forgiving place and if you get it wrong then your business is not going to succeed.

Happily, that is not going to happen to you because you are about to read this book. It contains twenty vital short cuts to help you create a successful business in the simplest and fastest way possible. Following them will save you a lot of time, a lot of frustration, a lot of pain and a lot of money. This book will open your eyes to aspects of starting up and running a business that you never thought about before and it will make you think twice about merely following the expected way of doing things. Best of all, it is full of fascinating and revealing stories about other entrepreneurs who have gone before you, so you can learn from their successes and also from their mistakes.

Of course, not everyone wants or chooses to start up a business solely in order to sell it. There are many other brilliant reasons for starting up a business. You might want to create a business that will provide a comfortable lifestyle for you and your family for many years to come. Or to build something of long-lasting worth that can eventually be passed down through the family from generation to generation. You might be aiming to create an enterprise with a social conscience which can be a blueprint for a whole new way of doing things. Or to build a business that will provide meaningful employment to a local community and give opportunities to people who would not otherwise have had access to them.

Well, this book is for you, too. It will show you how to build your business without wasting time and money along the way on pointless and unnecessary diversions, and get it to the point where it is stable enough and established enough to thrive and start fulfilling the aims you have for it, all in the fastest possible time. Time and energy are precious commodities and if I can help you to use them in the most effective way then I will consider it a job well done. Whatever your ultimate aim, there is a faster way to get there and this book will show you how.

Now, I'm not going to pretend for one minute that it's not still going to be hard work. It is tremendously hard starting up any kind of business from scratch and there is no guarantee of success, for anyone. It would be wrong for me to pretend otherwise. But at least this way, when you put the effort in, you will know that you are putting it into all the right places, and in the right way. And you will know that you have given both you and your business the very best chance of success.

There is another good reason why everyone wants to be an entrepreneur. It is because creating something from nothing and turning a good idea into a fortune has to be the most exciting thing you can ever do. To become an entrepreneur is to embark on a magical, thrilling, unpredictable, life-changing adventure. And if you get it right, the results can be truly spectacular. So if you can get there faster, so much the better. It just gives you more time to enjoy your success. See you on the beach.

CHAPTER 1

BEGIN AT THE END

The title of this book is *How to Make a Million before Lunch* – but actually a mere million doesn't even come close to what it could be. Wondering how much money you can really make starting up a business from scratch? Well, let's see. Lara Morgan started up her business Pacific Direct with £356, which she used to buy a fax machine. She sold the business, which sold toiletries to hotels, a few years later for £20 million. Maria Kempinska started her business Jongleurs, the chain of comedy venues, with just £300. She went on to sell the business for £8 million. And Gerry Pack started up Holiday Extras, providing hotel rooms and parking at airports, with just £100 and sold it in 2005 for £42 million.

You may not read about these kinds of business sales in the press because many of them are private deals for undisclosed sums – but, believe me, deals like this are happening every week. And one day your business could be one of them.

Now, remember, none of these businesses were doing anything particularly radical. They were selling shampoo, comedy entertainment and airport hotel rooms. And none of them were household names in the way that big businesses such as Tesco and B&Q are. You may have heard of Jongleurs and possibly Holiday Extras but you are unlikely to have heard of Pacific Direct. And yet for a small initial outlay of just a few hundred pounds, three ordinary people managed to achieve unimaginable wealth in the space of a few years. In the process they changed their lives and the lives of those around them. Simply by having an idea, following it through, working hard and then selling the business they had created. Sounds appealing?

Now for the basics. There are lots of reasons why people start businesses and all of them are equally valid. You may be doing it because you want to take control of your own life. Or because you are fed up with working for someone else and want to be your own boss. It may be because someone once told you that you would never amount to anything and you want to prove them wrong. Or because you want to buy a bigger house, or because you are stuck at home all day bringing up children and want something to think about other than potty-training and homework.

But whatever the reason for starting it up, if you sincerely want to make a serious amount of money from your business then at some point you have to sell it. The value you create in your business will remain largely locked inside that business until you find someone willing to crystallise that value by paying real money for it. What's more, you need to be thinking about selling it before you have even started it up.

It's all about selling it

Let's look at those two ideas in turn. First, the importance of selling your business. Yes, a business may provide you with a comfortable income and even the occasional dividend once it is properly established. But in order to unlock the true value in your business you really need to sell it. Indeed, many entrepreneurs never see a single penny from their business until they do sell it.

Ideally, what you want to do is to start making profits as soon as you can – some entrepreneurs manage to do this in the first month, many more within the first six months – because having a business which is profitable makes it easy for a buyer to put a value on it. Traditionally, the value of a private business is based on a multiple of between four and ten times its profits before interest and tax, depending on the sector it is in. It also gives a buyer the benefit of a ready income stream and confidence that they are buying something with a future.

But actually these days you don't have to be making profits already to be able to sell your business. You just have to show that it has the potential to do so one day.

Just look at the enormous prices paid in the past few years for some online businesses which at the time had yet to make any profits. Search engine company Google paid US$1.65 billion to buy video-sharing website YouTube in 2006 and online auctioneer eBay paid an eye-watering US$2.6 billion for Skype, the internet phone service, in 2005. Neither had ever made a profit up to that point.

But while your business doesn't need profits to entice a buyer, it does need potential. Bags of it. And this is why it is so important that you start thinking about the idea of selling your business almost as soon as you've had the idea for the business – because you need to structure it in the right way so that it will appeal to a prospective buyer. And that means showing off the potential of the business in the best possible light. And *that* means getting the framework right before you have even sold a single thing. It may sound extreme but actually it is vital, especially if time is of the essence. Good preparation can add a significant amount to the sale price – and could even determine whether or not you are able to sell your company at all.

Remember, selling a business is not the same as selling a house or a car – if the buyer doesn't feel comfortable with the business then they will not ask to reduce the price; they will simply decide not to buy and will walk away.

There are three rules for creating a business that someone might actually want to buy:

1. Find yourself a niche

Make your company as attractive as possible by giving it a focus and creating a niche, in other words a corner of the market in which it can really stand out and shine. Ideally you want to make it the best of its kind at what it does. Ask yourself what your business is going to be known for – what sets it apart from all the rest and is therefore worth paying a premium for?

2. Show there is potential for substantial future growth

No one wants to buy a business they feel has reached its peak. You can obviously show there is potential for strong future growth by writing a business plan which highlights where all the future profits can be made, for example in overseas markets, or by expanding into related products to complement the ones you already sell. But, even better, you can show the potential for growth by what your business actually does. Planning to start up an online business selling everything that cats need? It doesn't take a great leap of imagination to see that you could expand the format to include dogs, guinea pigs and, ultimately, all pets.

This is very much what first-time entrepreneur Wendy Shand has done. A few years ago she started her online business Tots to France, offering child-friendly holiday homes in France that had been inspected for safety and were kitted out with stair gates, high chairs and so on. She then expanded to Italy with Tots to Italy, and has now changed the name of the business to Tots to Travel because she has further expanded to include properties in Spain, Portugal and the UK – and, as she points out on her website, would eventually like to provide child-friendly properties all over the world.

3. Take yourself out of the business

To be able to sell your business you need to remove yourself from the daily running of the business, because otherwise you will remain a vital element of the company and you will never be able to sell it without you going along as part of the package. You need to delegate all your tasks within the company to other people, so that the business can function effectively on its own without you being involved. Basically you need to make yourself redundant. This is not something you will be able to do, or will want to do, instantly but it should be something that is constantly at the back of your mind.

This means that your business must be scalable. In other words, that you yourself do not actually have to be there to do the thing that makes the money. And therefore that growth is not limited to what you yourself can physically do. If the core of the business is centred around your particular skill – making beautiful, intricate stained-glass windows, for example, or writing complex computer software, then you are in big trouble right from the start, because:

▸▸ the business will never be able to grow beyond what you physically can do yourself, which in turn is limited by the fact that there are only twenty-four hours in a day and by your own personal stamina.

▸▸ a prospective buyer will only want to buy the business if you come along with it. Which will not only totally scupper your plans to spend the rest of your life sipping cocktails on a yacht, it will turn you into an employee, albeit a well-paid one, for the rest of your life, something that you were presumably trying to avoid by starting up your own business in the first place.

If it is a skill you can teach other people then of course that is fine – and if you can teach it to a computer, even better. Estate agents have been particularly ahead of the game in this area. Property-finding websites such as rightmove.co.uk and globrix.com can email you regular updates of properties for sale in your chosen area and at your chosen price, a far more efficient way of finding out what has just come on the market than having to call a dozen estate agents every day. And estate agents such as Foxtons and KFH now have interactive maps on their websites which show you at a glance exactly where all their properties for sale and for rent are located, a vast improvement on getting an estate agent to drive you around the area while you are trying to match up a pile of printed sales particulars and a battered *A to Z* street map.

Charlie Hoult, an entrepreneur who is now chief executive of brand agency Loewy, has sold two businesses in the past few years. One was a newsletter publishing company and the other a serviced office business. He believes the single most important factor in selling a company is to make sure the owner is not needed to run the business.

He says: 'Many entrepreneurs build their business round themselves, which makes it impossible to sell. But if you want to sell it, you need to be dispensable.'

Your business also needs to be one that a buyer easily understands and immediately grasps the concept of. In the image it portrays to the world, your business needs to do exactly what it says on the tin.

Good branding is vital

A key way of adding value to your business – and therefore of increasing the price that someone might want to pay for it – is to create a brand for it. A brand is initially about choosing a great name for your product or service. One that is easy to say and spell, does not mean anything rude in another language, and that is unique to you. It can either be a name that describes what the business does – classically brilliant brand names include Mothercare, Toys Я Us and Burger King – or you can choose a name which means nothing initially but which you hope to embellish with meaning as your business develops. Great examples of this include Starbucks, McDonald's and Domino's. The value embedded in a good brand name can easily add millions to the price someone is prepared to pay for it.

So too will a logo used alongside the brand – indeed, in some cases, instead of the brand. You only have to look at how much big businesses are prepared to pay to have their businesses rebranded, or even just tweaked. BP famously spent a fortune just to have the letters BP tilted to one side, and has since spent another fortune to add a sunflower and move it lower-case to bp. Successful logos include the Nike 'swoosh', the London Underground symbol and the McDonald's golden arches. You can tell they work when you don't need to ask what the logos stand for – you just know.

It can also go disastrously wrong, of course, which is why you need to take great care to get it right. The Post Office spent a lot of money changing its name to Consignia, and then just fourteen months later changed it back to the Post Office again.

But even if you get it right, branding is about more than simply finding an eye-catching name or a logo. You also need to create a strong identity for your business which runs through everything you do, so that the whole thing makes sense to outsiders. Let me explain. First of all you need to decide what kind of identity you want your company to have. Do you want to be seen as a funky, cutting-edge high-fashion business, for example, or would you prefer to be seen as solid, dependable and reliable? What is the core idea of the company? If you don't know what the company stands for it is difficult to create an identity. You can come up with the most amazing name and logo but if you have no vision or proposition for the company, it will fall apart.

Poundland is an almost perfect example of a company which has an easily understood core vision and brand. It is called Poundland and everything it sells costs one pound. It does exactly what the name implies and you even know in advance how much everything costs. Magic.

Here's how to create the right image for your business:

▶▶ Think about what kind of message you want your business to project

▶▶ Ask other people what they think

▶▶ Make sure the identity is consistent throughout every aspect of your business

9

▶▶ When you have chosen a new identity, ensure it is
continually monitored so that it remains relevant

You also need to think about the professional image you
portray. Don't hire a well-meaning friend to do your accounts
as a hobby in their spare time, for example. That is not a
good look at all for a business that is supposed to be destined
for great things. Employ an accountant who is already experienced in selling businesses, so he will not be fazed by
the idea, and who can guide you throughout the lifespan
of your company, and especially can advise how best to
organise your taxes – personal, corporate, capital gains – in
anticipation of a sale. Not only will it look far more impres-
sive to a potential buyer, it will be better for the business,
too.

Then learn to love your computer. A future buyer is going
to want to see detailed up-to-date databases of your customers,
so get the software you need to ensure you can start doing
this from day one. The same goes for having a clear set of
detailed accounts.

You also need to be very aware right from the beginning
of the importance of tying major customers and suppliers
into the business. Put in place long-term rolling contracts
with your key customers and suppliers so that a buyer feels
comfortable that they will remain in place when the business is under new ownership. Your buyer needs to be
reassured that the special secret ingredient that goes into
your cakes and has been the principal reason for their
demand is still going to be delivered every Monday when
they are in charge.

You see now why it is so important to start thinking about all this stuff before you have even started your business. It is a lot easier to think about having a focus and creating a niche and developing a brand when you have a blank piece of paper in front of you and all the possibilities in the world, than if you are belatedly trying to create a focus and a niche for a business that is already well established.

Who's the buyer?

Finally, you need to think about what kind of buyer might be interested in your business. It could be a rival keen to expand their market share; it could be a retailer who wants to expand into actually making products; or, equally, it could be a manufacturer keen to get a shop front – either on the high street or online – of their own.

In fact, if you are smart you may be able to work out which other specific firms are likely to want to buy your business before you've even started it. That way you can shape and structure your firm in a way that is most likely to appeal to the buyer you have identified – by going into markets where they are not, but would like to be, or else having operations that dovetail nicely with where they currently operate. Get a piece of paper and write down actual names.

It is worth spending some time thinking about how to bag a trade buyer because, if you can find a buyer who needs your business to fill in a missing piece of the jigsaw, they are likely to be happy to pay several times more than your business is worth on a strictly accounting valuation. If you are able to find a buyer such as a foreign company wanting an outlet in the country in which you are located, for example, or you manage to find a company in the north that wants to get a foothold in the south, then you must not let them get away as they will be basing their valuation not on how much your business is strictly worth, but on how much it would cost them – in time, effort and money – to start up a similar operation themselves.

The other big benefit of selling your business to a trade buyer, as opposed to a private equity firm or venture capitalist, is that the former can't wait to get you out of the door once the sale is completed so that they can start running the business their own way. On the other hand, a private equity firm or venture capitalist is likely to want you to stay running the business for a while after the deal is done, for at least three years and possibly five. And, worse, they are likely to include a hefty earn-out clause which means you only get the money if you meet certain targets – and you forfeit a shed load of the selling price if you quit early.

Remember, you only get the chance to sell your business once, so make sure you get it right. Then all you have to start worrying about is how to spend the money you have made.

ACTION PLAN

▶▶ Decide what your niche is. What is your business going to be doing that is special and different?

▶▶ Draw up a list of big firms operating in your industry sector that you think might want to buy your business in the future. If you don't think a particular firm would be interested, ask yourself why not. If it is something about the structure of your business that might put them off – perhaps you will be opening in the wrong area, for example, or targeting the wrong kind of customers – then it is worth thinking about whether you should be changing your approach.

▶▶ Look closely at your business model and make sure it is scalable. In other words, can it grow without you being there? If the answer is no, it is a non-starter. Think of a new idea.

CHAPTER 2

DO SOMETHING YOU REALLY UNDERSTAND

Long before Simon Cowell became well known as an acerbic talent show judge, he started up a record label called Fanfare. It had a few hits but Simon quickly realised that to be successful in the long term he would need to know more about the music industry. So he found himself a mentor – record producer and fellow *Pop Idol* judge Pete Waterman, who had helped him to produce a hit record by the singer Sinitta.

Simon says: 'I followed him around for three years like a dog. I would follow him into meetings and watch him in the studio. I remember him turning to me one day and saying, "Simon, why are you following me around?" But it was an invaluable experience. I learnt an awful lot from him.'

If you want to create a million-pound business from scratch in the shortest possible time, there is one very obvious thing you should do. Do something you know about. This is blindingly obvious advice and I feel almost embarrassed writing it. But it is truly amazing how many people jump into starting a business with two feet first and eyes closed having absolutely no experience at all of the industry they are entering. I am forever meeting fledgling entrepreneurs at conferences who tell me about the business they plan to set up – and then cheerfully, almost as an afterthought, admit they have no prior knowledge of the industry they are trying to break into and say things like, 'Oh I haven't got the faintest idea what I am doing.'

I can totally understand the thinking behind it. When you are stuck in a dead-end job, hating every minute of it, there can be a huge temptation to go off and do something completely different, to throw yourself in at the deep end somewhere and see what happens. In a purely abstract way, the idea of jumping into the unknown without a lifebelt can be exhilarating.

But starting up a business from scratch is hard enough without making it any more difficult. If you want to do something completely different there are all manner of things you can easily do without remortgaging your house and putting your family's livelihood on the line first – scuba-diving, for example, or pot-holing, or learning how to cook Chinese food. In fact, if you did something such as scuba-diving you would learn how to do it first before gaily plunging to the bottom of the ocean. You should treat starting a business in the same way.

Use everything you have learnt

When Jan Ward started up her business Corrotherm
International, which sells non-corrosive pipes that can withstand high temperatures to oil and gas firms around the
world, she didn't do it because it was glamorous or because
it involved foreign travel. She did it because she knew all
about non-corrosive pipes. She knew everything there was
to know about them and everything there was to know about
the industry and the market she was selling into. And that
was because she had spent the previous ten years working
for two businesses which had been doing exactly the same
thing. As a result Jan even knew exactly where there was a
gap in the market and how best she could fill it with her
new business. Frankly, if she hadn't been successful, it would
have been a bit of a surprise.

As she says: 'If you are going to do anything you really
have to know the industry to be successful. I was doing
something that was very familiar and I was dealing with
customers and suppliers that were very familiar to me, and
I knew how to set up a company. I had learnt all those
lessons so I wasn't doing anything that I didn't know about.'
As a result her business now has sales of more than £10
million.

Andrew Crawford adopted a similar approach. When he
decided to start up an online bookselling business, he was
extremely well qualified to do so, having already spent several
years working for two other online booksellers. First he
worked for a small company called Book Pages, which sold

books over the internet when the medium was still in its formative stages. Then, when Amazon bought out the company to use as a base to set up its British arm, he worked for Amazon, spending three years learning everything he could about how the business operated, ending up as Senior Operations Director.

By the time he was twenty-nine, Andrew had amassed a wealth of experience about the online book market and had worked out that there was room for a competitor in that market.

Under the terms of his contract with Amazon, he was forbidden to start up a competing business straight away so initially he became a consultant for start-up companies. But by 2004 he was free to follow his dream and so, with £10,000 of his own savings, he built a website and The Book Depository was born.

The business has a single, simple aim – to try to make all books available to all people. In order to differentiate himself from the competition, Andrew introduced another enticement – free delivery to anywhere in the world, for even a single book. 'You can buy a 20p book on our site and we will deliver it to Australia free,' he says. 'We are very good at supply chain and we worked out that we can afford to do this.'

His instincts were spot-on. In the first year The Book Depository had sales of £2.2 million and was profitable from the first month. By the second year sales had risen to £11 million. Andrew also started a publishing programme in which the firm republished two hundred titles that were out of copyright and out of print.

Even better, despite having left Amazon to do his own thing,

Andrew continued to have close ties with the company, to the extent that customers on his site are offered the choice of buying a book through The Book Depository site or through Amazon.

'We complement Amazon in some ways because we provide the books that they can't get hold of that easily,' he says. The philosophy has paid off in spades. The company's annual turnover is now more than £35 million.

Andrew is clear about the secret of his success. 'For me it is having an intimate knowledge of the book supply chain. I have been doing this for ten years, so I am very experienced in it.'

Spot the gap in the market

Phil Langley's job enabled him to spot a gap in the market in his particular industry which someone coming into the industry from the outside would have been hard-pushed to discover.

Phil sold water coolers that dispensed water from bottles, which were replaced when the previous bottles became empty. When the company acquired another business in 2001, it came with a division that supplied machines that took water from the mains and cooled and filtered it before dispensing it.

Phil was asked to look at what should be done with this division. He started researching the market and discovered that mains-fed coolers had several advantages over bottle-fed ones, not least because they did not require someone to deliver full bottles of water and take away the empty ones. Cutting out the transport element also made the product greener.

The central problem faced by the existing players in the

market was that customers did not want to go to the effort and expense of installing the plumbing that was needed for a mains-fed machine.

Phil realised that this hurdle could be overcome by offering plumbing as part of the deal, and reported his findings to his boss. 'I said you have a great opportunity here. If you don't enter this market, you are going to lose all your high-volume clients to mains-fed water dispensing.'

His employers were, however, reluctant to commit to mains-fed coolers because they had already invested millions of pounds in bottled-water dispensers.

So, in 2002, at the age of twenty-six, Langley decided to do it himself. He resigned from his job and got a £100,000 bank loan. From the start he decided to rent out the machines to businesses on long-term service contracts. He negotiated a deal with a provider to supply and maintain his water coolers and hired two salespeople.

Then he got to work trying to find customers, hoping to entice them by including plumbing in the deal. It was hard work but he persevered and the business, Premier Water-coolers, now has a turnover of more than £3.5 million and employs fifty people.

Gain the knowledge you need at someone else's expense

But what if you really don't have experience of anything useful that could possibly form the basis of a new business? What if your job is in an industry so tedious that you couldn't bear to have anything further to do with it? Your first task must to be to go out and get the experience you need – at someone else's expense. Think about it. If you can get the experience you need by working for someone else first, you will save yourself a fortune by avoiding all the mistakes you might have made using your own money.

This, of course, is where you need to swallow your pride and your vanity, fast. Because to get the experience you need you are very likely going to have to work at the very bottom rung of your chosen industry, probably for minimal pay and possibly even for no pay at all. It can take guts to give up a well-paid office job and voluntarily go and work in a sandwich bar, or a clothes factory or estate agent, for a while, even when you yourself know why you are doing it. It can also be annoying to have to spend a few weeks or more doing some menial task when you are itching to get going with starting up your own business. But it can pay dividends.

Russel Coultart had a high-flying career as the director of an insurance company. However he longed to start up a record label so at the age of thirty he quit his job and chose to go and work as an unpaid tea boy in a recording studio in the East End of London for eighteen months, solely to learn how the industry worked.

He says: 'I was on the dole and I lived hand-to-mouth. It was a case of wondering whether I could afford to buy a loaf of bread. But I learnt how to make records.'

It was only when he felt he knew enough that he left to start up a record label of his own. It was a success and when Russel started selling his records via the internet his business, now called Digital Stores, really took off and today has an annual turnover of £6 million.

Another way of learning how to be an entrepreneur, of course, is to go and work for one. That way you get to see what growing a business is like from the inside. This is what Nick Rutter did.

Before he started up his business Fire Angel, which makes fire alarms and other fire safety equipment, he spent two years in Hong Kong working for a local entrepreneur there called Joseph Wong, who made plastic electronic toys for children.

Nick says: 'Hong Kong was a big epiphany for me. The entrepreneurial spirit I had had as a kid had been knocked out of me a bit by that stage.' It was not long, however, before being in Hong Kong helped him to find it again – and to realise that he too had the potential to be a successful entrepreneur.

He says: 'In Hong Kong these guys were not superhuman, but they just got on with it.' After a month, his boss invited him to come for a ride on his boat. 'I remember pulling out of the harbour on this 60-foot yacht, thinking OK, this is good.'

Indeed, his time in Hong Kong not only helped him rekindle his entrepreneurial spirit, it also ended up shaping the type of business he decided to start up himself. The first product he and his business partner, Sam Tate, launched was a plug-in smoke alarm with rechargeable batteries – a plastic electronic product which he had made in China. The business now has a turnover of more than £14 million a year.

You don't have time to learn on the job

Many businesses fail because in the time it took for the owner to learn about how the industry worked, the business was going under. Whereas in the past customers might have been tolerant of a business that let them down or got things wrong, or forgot a delivery or messed up an order, these days the huge availability of other options means that when a business goes down, it goes down fast. The commercial world is not a forgiving place in which to make mistakes.

There is nothing cool about losing large amounts of money simply because you didn't know what you were doing. And the advantages of being your own secret squirrel cannot be overestimated. As we all know from watching Gordon Ramsay's television show *Ramsay's Kitchen Nightmares*, which lifted the lid on failing restaurants, things often look very different behind the scenes of a business than they do upfront. It is while you are cleaning the toilets or sweeping the floor that you will discover the dark secrets of the industry you are trying to enter. And then how your business can do it all differently and run off with all the customers.

Get your overalls on

I have done several fairly menial but revealing jobs in my life. I once spent a summer working for a British holiday company on a campsite in France, where customers stayed in mobile homes or tents. It was my job to welcome them, to clean their accommodation before they arrived and to look after them during their stay. As well as the firm I worked for, there was also its main competitor, another British holiday firm, operating at the site.

It quickly became apparent that although on the face of it the two companies looked very similar in terms of their glossy brochures and their prices, in reality there was a gulf a mile wide between the two businesses. The company I worked for didn't have any of the spare equipment we were supposed to have, so whenever a customer asked for something that was missing or whenever something broke – as often happened – my colleagues and I would have to beg, borrow or steal it from our competitors, whether it was a spare cooker, some games equipment or a chair.

Our rivals meanwhile had store cupboards full of brand-new equipment which they would produce the minute a customer needed it, while we could only look on in envy.

It was quite obvious to us employees that while our firm was quite clearly operating on an inefficient shoestring, our competitors were well funded and all geared up to increase their presence in the market. All that bartering made for a highly entertaining – if sometimes infuriating – summer for us, but imagine how useful that kind of information would be to an entrepreneur who was thinking of entering the same market themselves.

There are a hundred other ways to gain the knowledge you need before plunging head first into a business. Go to industry trade fairs and talk to as many people as you can: existing players in the industry and, even better, potential customers and suppliers. Go to business networking events and spend hours trawling the internet for industry insights and market data. You will be amazed at what you can find if you look hard enough. But the key thing is to do all of this before you actually launch the business because, once you are up and running, you won't have time to think, let alone learn, and any lack of knowledge will slow you down and cause you to make silly, possibly costly, mistakes.

Ask yourself why you are starting a business in an area you know nothing about anyway. What are you hoping to gain from doing it that way? If it is excitement and the thrill of the challenge that you crave, then take six months out to travel the world first and get all that out of your system. Remember, this is not a 'now or never' call that you are making here – make a success of your first business doing something that you know about, and then you will have bought yourself the freedom to do something a bit more adventurous the second or third time around.

Put away your passport

That goes for starting up a business overseas, too. At first glance the idea of opening a bar on a beach in the south of France, or the Caribbean, sounds much more appealing than opening one in Solihull or Scunthorpe (with apologies to Solihull and Scunthorpe). But think again. Starting a business overseas instead of at home instantly quadruples your chances of failure, if you haven't spent a considerable amount of time living there first – and even if you have. All the things you take for granted here – about how things work and how the infrastructure is organised, and indeed even the concept of becoming an entrepreneur – may well be different elsewhere. And the problems of trying to understand the red tape and bureaucracy involved will inevitably be immense and enormously time-consuming.

A lot of people have written books about the hilarity of trying to get anything done in Italy, or Spain, or wherever, when the locals have different ideas about time and deadlines. And it can be great fun reading about the perils of olive farming in Italy, or attempting to open a bed and breakfast in France, from the comfort of your armchair.

But if you truly want to start and maintain a successful business and not simply give yourself the material for a book, then take my advice and stay at home.

Hobby into business might not go

I am often asked if one should try and turn a hobby into a business and it's not an easy question to answer. The big advantage of a hobby, of course, is that it is something you know a lot about and enjoy doing, and those are two very big plus points. And some people do make a huge success of turning their hobby into a commercial business. Helen Colley, for example, spent years making puddings purely for pleasure before starting up a business producing traditional sticky toffee puddings in the kitchen of her parents' farmhouse. She sold her business, Farmhouse Fare, for £10 million in 2006.

But for others it could potentially be a disastrous move. If you enjoy your hobby precisely because it is an escape from your day-to-day reality and is something you really can do for pure pleasure – whether that be keeping bees or designing your own greetings cards – then you need to think hard about whether you will still enjoy doing it when you have to do it all day, every day, even when you really don't feel like it. It is worth remembering, too, that trying to make money out of something can change the whole nature of it. If you have always loved giving your handmade socks as presents, for example, or making jam for the annual village fete, then charging for those things can take away a lot of that pleasure.

One way of finding out how you really feel about this is to take two weeks off work – or out of your life, if you have been made redundant – and do your hobby as if it were your job every day from morning till night. If you can't stand the sight of your workshop/kitchen/bees at the end of the fortnight, then you have your answer.

ACTION PLAN

▶▶ Look at your CV. Is there any knowledge you have gained that might be useful for starting up a business? Was there any job where you thought, I can do better than this company is doing? Was there any gap in the market which you thought needed filling?

▶▶ Get a part-time position in the industry you wish to enter. You can do this to fit round your current job, if you have one. Not only will this give you a greater insight into the industry, it will also help you decide if this is something you really want to do.

▶▶ Subscribe to all the trade magazines covering your industry and immerse yourself in them.

CHAPTER 3

MOVE AWAY FROM THE PENCIL – LEAVE THE INVENTIONS TO SOMEONE ELSE

I want to tell you a cautionary tale. A few years ago I met a would-be entrepreneur, a lovely man who we shall call Hamish. Hamish was in his early thirties and was full of enthusiasm for a business idea he firmly believed was going to make him extremely rich. He told me he had been working on an invention, something to do with technology. He was very excited about his project and spent every waking hour working away at his computer.

Even at the time it seemed like a rather ambitious venture for someone to be working on alone, given that Bill Gates and Steve Jobs and half the firms in Silicon Valley probably had hundreds of people working on solving exactly the same problem.

But Hamish was so committed that nothing would stand in the way of his dream. He hired a patent attorney at huge cost to help him take out a string of patents for his project; he endlessly pitched his idea to investors and talked confidently about the imminent launch of the business.

That was eight years ago. I met Hamish again recently and he was a shadow of his former self. It quickly emerged that his business was still not yet launched, partly because getting his invention to work had proved far more difficult and complex than he initially thought, and partly because getting all the patents needed to protect his idea in place had drained him of time and energy as well as money.

Also, there was the rather large problem that, during the eight years that Hamish had been working on his project, technology in the area he was working on had advanced anyway and so his invention was looking less and less relevant by the week.

As a result he was now personally £150,000 in debt and was living in people's spare rooms. His relationship with his girlfriend had collapsed, he could not sleep at night for worrying and he was suffering from permanent exhaustion.

This, I hardly need tell you, is not the way to become a successful entrepreneur.

One of the most common misconceptions among would-be entrepreneurs – fuelled, incidentally, by television programmes such as *Dragons' Den* – a BBC television series in which entrepreneurs pitch to a panel of judges who then decide whether or not to invest their own money in a project – is that to create a successful business you need to invent a product that is completely and entirely new. I have lost count of the number of phone calls and emails I have received from would-be entrepreneurs telling me about their brilliant idea for a new kitchen implement or a new gardening tool or whatever, and asking my advice on how to go about turning their idea into a multi-million-pound business. No doubt to their great disappointment, my advice is always the same: DON'T DO IT. Put the pencil down, tear up the piece of paper and walk away from the kitchen. If you proceed with your plan you might as well throw all your money in the bin and tear your hair out in frustration right now, because that is undoubtedly what you will end up doing.

The good news is that you don't actually have to invent anything in order to make a million. Successful businesses are often based on incredibly simple ideas and yours can be, too.

Take a look at how the Dragons made their fortunes and you will begin to see what I mean. Peter Jones made his money from selling mobile phones, Duncan Bannatyne made his money from opening nursing homes and then gyms, Theo Paphitis from selling stationery and women's lingerie. Deborah Meaden made her fortune from caravan parks and James Caan made his money by setting up a recruitment firm.

Not exactly rocket science, any of their money-making ideas, are they? Indeed, the first thing that strikes you is just how mundane their business ideas are, and how many times they have been done before and since. The second thing that should strike you is that, because all these ideas were already in existence, they had a ready market of people willing to buy them. The only difference between those other people selling mobile phones and stationery and opening gyms was that the Dragons did it slightly better, or more effectively, or in a more efficient way.

Don't get me wrong. I am not against people inventing things. Inventions are what make the world go round and life would undoubtedly be a much duller place without iPods, non-stick pans and toys that glow in the dark. But inventing things is not a game for first-time entrepreneurs. It takes years and years to get an invention from the drawing board to the shelves of Tesco or B&Q and it requires far too much risk and pain for someone who is financing it by remortgaging the family home and feeding the kids baked beans on toast for a year.

The inventor reality

Let's take a look at what would need to happen in order for your invention to make you a million pounds. First, you would need to make a prototype to prove that it actually works. That is likely to set you back a few thousand pounds straight away, depending on the complexity of the invention. Then you will need to protect your idea by getting it patented, meaning that no one else is allowed to copy it for twenty years. You apply for a patent by submitting diagrams and explanations to the Intellectual Property Office. The first step, applying for one, is fairly straightforward. Unfortunately, the next step, actually getting a patent granted, is not. It can take up to four years to get a patent granted and it can be fearsomely complicated to get it right so you are likely to need to hire patent lawyers to help you, and their fees will run into thousands of pounds. You can begin to market your product before the patent is finally granted by putting the words 'patent pending' on your product, but again you are going to need expensive advice to go down this path.

Depending on what your product is, you might then try to interest a high street retailer in your product. If the retailer likes your product, it may offer you either a licensing deal, in which you receive a royalty for each product sold, or a lump sum to buy your product idea outright. The bad news is that this whole process takes up another huge chunk of time.

Even assuming you struck lucky early on and did not have to have dozens of meetings with potential retailers, you must be prepared to wait a long time before you see your product in a catalogue or on the shelves – typically up to eighteen months. Actually getting any money from anything that is sold could be another six months after that.

Keep it simple

Now let's look at what happens if you decide not to invent your own product but to start up a business selling someone else's products instead. Setting up a website with e-commerce facilities can be done in the space of a few days – and so can ordering in supplies of products. Which means you can be pretty much up and running within a week. OK, realistically a few weeks. But a few weeks compared to up to six years? Hmm, a difficult one.

Now let's have a quiz. Name all the successful modern inventors in this country who have made money from their inventions. Ready to show your answers? The chances are you will come up with two names at most – James Dyson and Trevor Baylis. Brilliant inventors, both spent years and years banging their heads against brick walls trying to turn their inventions into commercial products. Still convinced that invention is the way forward?

Find a proven idea then make it better

So if you are not going to create a new product to make your fortune, what are you going to do? The answer is to sell a product or service that already exists, for which there is a known and proven demand. Then aim to improve on the way that product or service is currently being offered to customers. Make your product faster, or more robust, or more environmentally friendly than the competition. Make your service better or more efficient, or more accessible. Sell it in a different way. Make people want to buy one of your products rather than the one they could get from your competitor.

If you are stuck for ideas, just look around you. If everything in your life works smoothly and perfectly every time then I cannot help you. But if, as I suspect is the case, there are little things about the way the world works that constantly drive you mad and infuriate you, then here is your inspiration. Do all the dry-cleaners in your town close at 5 p.m.

and never open at weekends? Start one that stays open late and every day of the week. Is your favourite shampoo only available in an obscure shop miles out of town? Sell it online. Finding it impossible to get a good builder? Start up a network of trustworthy tradesmen based on word-of-mouth recommendations. There are a million more opportunities like this without you ever having to invent a thing.

Martyn Dawes is a first-time entrepreneur who made a fortune from selling coffee from vending machines. A real fortune, too – he sold his business, Coffee Nation, in 2008 for £20 million. His idea was blindingly simple – to provide vending machines which made better coffee than people could make themselves. After some trial and error he managed to do just that, getting his vending machines to make coffee using real coffee beans and fresh milk. Brilliantly simple, brilliantly successful.

Remember, entrepreneurial success is not about spending years in a shed making prototypes out of cardboard and sticky-backed plastic; it is about taking something that already exists and giving people a reason to buy it by making it better, cheaper, faster, simpler or more efficient. That way you will have a ready-made market for it and therefore a ready-made group of potential customers wanting to buy your product or service. If you really want to invent something from scratch, wait until you have made your millions and do it then, when you can afford to take your time over it and make mistakes and lose money.

One of my favourite entrepreneurs is Tim Roupell, because he has made a fortune out of seemingly the simplest thing of all – the sandwich. Tim used to work as a trader for a financial firm in the City but decided to start up a business making sandwiches largely because he was totally unskilled or unqualified to do anything else. To start with he sold his sandwiches from a basket which he took round offices himself each day and for the first few months he felt acutely embarrassed that he was trying to make a living out of doing something so simple. But he stuck at it and the business grew. He eventually sold the business in 2008 for several million pounds.

What is so endearing and inspiring about Tim's story is that it shows that it really is possible to do something as staggeringly simple as making sandwiches and still make a fortune from selling the business a few years later. They are in no way revolutionary or ground-breaking sandwiches, and they look much like any other pre-packed triangular sandwich. Tim did not have any shops and the only time he tried opening one he closed it down after six weeks because it was an unnecessary complication to the business. Where his skill lay was in selling his sandwiches to the right people at the right price and delivering them on time – and keeping his costs low enough so that he could make a decent profit on the deal. Again, not rocket science, certainly, but who needs rocket science when there is a multi-million-pound fortune to be made?

You can still be creative

Basing your business on something that already exists does not mean that you can't still be creative. Step forward Phil Vecht, who started up his company Admedia in 2007. Phil was at a conference one day when he suddenly had a brainwave – why not put adverts up in washrooms, above urinals and on the back of toilet doors? It was a brilliantly simple idea. Advertisers would have the undivided attention of a captive audience and could even tailor their adverts for a gender-specific audience. It was such a simple idea that Phil could not believe it had not been done before and he actually spent quite a lot of time carefully researching it to find out if there was a fatal flaw he had missed.

But there wasn't and he discovered that advertisers were delighted to have found a new place to advertise, and landlords of places such as shopping centres and motorway service stations were delighted to have found a new source of revenue.

It was a win-win-win situation, and a straightforward business model that simply involved bringing together advertisers and landlords. Phil Vecht now operates more than 22,000 poster sites in shopping centres, motorway service stations, bars, pubs and fitness clubs across the UK and his company currently has sales of £7 million a year.

It is instructive to look at lists of successful entrepreneurs and analyse exactly how they made their money. Take *The Sunday Times* Fast Track 100, for example, an annual list of the fastest-growing private companies in the UK. The top ten companies on the list in 2009 were proof that focusing on providing a better service, rather than invention, pays off. They included Cyclescheme, a company which administers a cycle-to-work scheme, Gio-Goi, a fashion wholesaler, Oxygen, a recruitment company, Mattressman, which sells mattresses, and Ella's Kitchen, which makes food for babies and toddlers.

I'm going to end this chapter with one of those ideas that makes you want to hit yourself on the head with a frying pan and shout, now why didn't I think of that? Michael Parker had the idea for his online business selling old-fashioned sweets, A Quarter Of, while having a pint in the pub with his brother. He realised that many of the old-fashioned sweets we used to eat as kids – things such as sherbet fountains, flying saucers and space dust – were still being made, and thought that if he liked the idea of being able to try them again then other people might too.

Inspired by memories of the corner sweet shop where he grew up, Michael designed his website with a free software programme from a disk stuck to the front of a magazine and started up the business with just £200, of which £80 was spent on buying his first stock of sweets. Fuelled by a wave of nostalgia, his business, which he wholly owns, now stocks more than seven hundred sweet varieties, after Michael managed to track down the original sweet manufacturers around the world. And it has an annual turnover of more than £3 million.

Now that's how to do it.

ACTION PLAN

▶▶ Every time you buy a product or use a
service, ask yourself why you are buying
this one and not a rival one. What is its
unique selling point that hooked you in?

▶▶ Write a list of the things that annoy and
frustrate you in life. Now write down what
would need to be done to stop them
annoying and frustrating you.

▶▶ Read as much as you can about
successful businesses and how they work.
Try to discover or work out what was the
core central idea around which the
business was based.

▶▶ Keep a notebook with you at all times.
Every time you think of an idea for a
business, or see something you could do
better, write it down immediately.
Otherwise it will fall straight out of your
head.

CHAPTER 4

MAKE SURE THERE IS A DEMAND FOR YOUR IDEA

When the caterer Prue Leith started her first business, she had it all planned out. Prue, who was brought up in South Africa and only discovered her love of food while working as an au pair in Paris at the age of twenty-one, decided she would make and deliver food to actors in their dressing rooms between the matinee and evening shows, and she would call her business Matinee Collations.

Unfortunately, there was a small but critical flaw in her plan. There was no demand for her product. In her excitement in setting up the business she had neglected to find out if actors actually wanted to eat between shows, or even if they liked to stay in their dressing rooms. As it turned

41

out, they didn't. During shows, it seemed, actors generally much preferred to go for a walk or go to the pub. If Prue had actually bothered to ask them before she embarked on her venture, she would have found this out and saved herself a lot of time, effort and expense. But she didn't and so the business folded after a few weeks.

This may sound blindingly obvious but, before you take any steps at all towards starting your business, make absolutely sure that there is a demand for the product or service you are planning to sell. I am constantly astounded at how few people actually do this before making life-changing decisions such as quitting their jobs and remortgaging their houses before jumping in feet first. Somehow in the excitement the most important question of all gets overlooked.

The problem is that many would-be entrepreneurs approach the question the wrong way. Instead of taking as their starting point the question of what it is that people want and need and what they would be prepared to pay for, the would-be entrepreneur starts by thinking about what it is that *they* want to do. Only then do they get round to thinking about whether anyone would like to buy whatever it is they want to sell. Often, tragically, thinking about this last bit comes far too late in the game. If, indeed, at all.

Don't try to create a new market from scratch

Not long ago a new restaurant opened in my neighbourhood selling upmarket kebabs to be eaten as a sit-down meal. The kebabs were made from high-quality organic ingredients and cost a lot more than your typical late-night doner kebab, and the restaurant's décor was tasteful and designer-led with brightly coloured cushions and murals.

The owner told me he was hoping to change the perception widely held among people in Britain that kebabs were something you ate from a dodgy shop – or, worse, a van – at 2 a.m. on the way home after a good night out. He wanted to persuade families that a kebab was something they might go out to eat for an evening meal or Sunday lunch in a restaurant.

It was no doubt a very honourable idea and a well-intentioned mission, but in my view it was far too bold and overambitious for a first-time entrepreneur. Changing people's attitudes to the way they eat things takes time, money, effort and good connections, none of which a first-time entrepreneur usually has.

Sadly and predictably, the people living in the area did not suddenly change their perception of kebabs. They did not suddenly start going to the restaurant for Sunday lunch. In fact, the restaurant never attracted more than a handful of customers and closed just six months after it opened.

Remember, this is your first business. You are entering a world you have only ever observed from the outside. Things are going to be hard enough without you needlessly making them any harder. Make your millions with a product that people actually want first and if at that point you are still convinced there is untapped demand out there for something else, then by all means go ahead.

And don't kid yourself that you are going to be able to create a new market from scratch and unearth a hitherto unsuspected need for your product. Yes, Steve Jobs managed to do it with the iPod but he already had a lifetime of experience of making and selling consumer products such as Apple Mac computers behind him. And we the consumers had, anyway, been busy getting used to the idea of sound and music on the move with the Sony Walkman and portable CD players. So by the time he was ready for the iPod so were we. And remember: as well as the knowledge he had already gained, Jobs had a whole support team of designers, technicians, marketers and so on to help him. You haven't.

Never forget that for every Steve Jobs with his iPod there is a Sir Clive Sinclair and his ill-fated C5 electric car. Yes, it got masses of publicity and back in 1985 everyone was talking about it and discussing whether it was the future of driving and so on, but did everyone buy one? No. He sold 12,000 of them and that was it. As a result Sir Clive lost a lot of money pursuing his dream.

Actually, if you take a look at a C5 now it is blindingly obvious why no one wanted one. I saw one at the Brooklands Museum in Surrey and apart from the impracticality of having to plug it in somewhere and charge it up every fifteen miles, the thing that instantly struck me was just how very tiny it was. Once you got in it you were practically sitting on the ground, with your hands down by your legs to steer it with a set of handlebars. And this was something you were supposed to drive on the main road alongside cars and lorries and buses that were many times bigger than you. And somehow hope that you wouldn't get squashed when they couldn't even see that you were there in the first place.

Do it better, do it faster

Rachel Stacey discovered the hard way that a product or service without a market is no way to proceed. When she started up her own business Mind the Gap Solutions in 2006, offering quality assurance and due diligence services for manufacturing firms, she was full of optimism that it would be a huge success.

Rachel, who ran the business from her home in north Lincolnshire, had previously worked for a supermarket chain doing quality assurance and hoped to sign up around ten companies and work with them for a month each throughout the course of the year.

Unfortunately, what she did not appreciate was that, even though she herself knew that firms needed to do quality assurance, it was not something the firms themselves felt the need for.

She says: 'Trying to get some companies to realise that they should be doing it was a bigger challenge that I had anticipated.'

The gap in the market turned out to be just an illusion, and two years after starting up the business Stacey had to close it down, losing her entire start-up capital of £10,000, which she had raised by remortgaging her flat.

She now works for someone else, but dreams of starting another business one day.

There are two things to learn from this:

▶▶ Without demand, you don't have a business

▶▶ Just because you think something is important
doesn't mean that other people will agree

As a first-time entrepreneur, the only time you should be
thinking about selling a product without an existing market
to sell it into is if you have discovered a product in another
country which is doing well there and you think could work
well here too. Harry Cragoe did this with great success with
the smoothie, a blended fruit drink he had discovered while
working in California but which was at the time completely
unknown in the UK. He decided to set up a business, PJ
Smoothies, to sell smoothies in the UK, and trading went
so well that ten years later he sold the company to PepsiCo
for £23 million. Adopting an idea you have seen in action
overseas does not always work as well as this, however, and
for every success story there are countless other failures, often
because the entrepreneur has underestimated the importance
of culture and climate on people's buying decisions. I have
lost track of the number of successful entrepreneurs who
told me they had looked at the idea of selling frozen yoghurt
in the UK – after seeing the huge demand for it in the US
– but eventually decided against it because of the vagaries
of the British climate. And looking out now at the driving
rain, I can see why. Selling frozen yoghurt in the UK could
still turn out to be a goldmine for some entrepreneur one
day, but as yet the potential upside remains unknown and
the potential pitfalls all too obvious.

The key to all this is to find a product which already exists
and for which there is already a market – and then do it
better. With people increasingly time-strapped these days,

there is a potentially huge market in simply doing existing things faster, for example. The classic example is Kwik Fit, which will change exhausts and tyres on the spot without an appointment. They are simply doing what garages up and down the country have been doing for years, but by doing it more quickly and efficiently and with more convenience to the customer they have managed to take a large share of the market.

Moneysupermarket.com is another great example of providing a service which already existed – that is, getting home insurance or car insurance – but making it faster and more efficient, by letting people input their details once only and then giving them quotes from dozens of insurance firms so they don't have to spend hours ringing round everyone. Incidentally, it is no coincidence that both these examples have made a success out of speeding up something which is intrinsically boring and a necessity which people would rather not do. Anything that makes life less painful and less annoying for people, and speeds up getting through the dull stuff so there is more time for the fun stuff, is a fantastic place to start looking for ideas.

Research, research, research

Which brings us to market research. This is what market research is not: asking your family what they think, quizzing your friends. Market research is also not, for first-timers, something that should be left entirely to instinct. Yes, instinct and gut feel play a vital role in guiding you to make the right decisions, and many seasoned entrepreneurs talk airily about the importance of gut instinct and how they run their lives and businesses by it. But for a first-timer risking your home and livelihood you need to back up your instinct with a bit more knowledge about both the market you are hoping to enter and the people you think are going to be buying your product.

The first thing you need to do is closely analyse the market you want to break into. Ask yourself, is there actually room in there for me? And, if so, where exactly? Look at what other products are currently being sold and at what level they are pitching themselves, and where your product or service might fit in. Let's take shoes as an example. It is possible to buy shoes at an enormously wide range of price and quality from places like Shoe Zone at one end of the scale, where slippers cost £5, through to shoe designers like Christian Louboutin, where shoes cost upwards of £250 a pair. Decide where you fit in and who you will be competing against – and what you will be doing better so that people will start buying shoes from you instead of the competition. You can, of course, go in at a much higher or lower price than the current spread of possibilities offered in your market, but it is useful to be aware of where you are going to fit in and why. And who is above and below you in terms of price and quality.

You know what I'm going to say next – get out there and ask your potential customers for their views on what you want to sell them. You don't have to stand outside a train station with a clipboard. In fact, unless you plan to sell your product outside train stations, that's not a great idea anyway as people are usually in far too much of a rush to give a considered response. Go to where you think your customers are most likely to be – in the gym, for example, if you are creating a health drink, or in the mother and toddlers playgroup if you are creating a baby product – and then chat to them casually. Your research won't be quantitative, but it will be qualitative and it will give you enough information either to support or demolish your gut feeling. Then at that point you can start to get some quantitative research, by asking one hundred or two hundred people whether they would buy your product, and, crucially, how much they would be prepared to pay it for.

Be as inventive as you like. When three friends from university wanted to find out what people thought of their pulped fruit drink they set up a stand at a local jazz festival and put two bins outside it. Customers were asked to vote on whether the budding entrepreneurs should give up their jobs to make their drinks full time by throwing their empty bottles into either a bin marked 'Yes' or one marked 'No'. By the end of the weekend the 'Yes' bin was overflowing and the three friends went on to found Innocent Smoothies, which then grew so fast that by 2009 they were able to sell a stake of between 15 and 20 per cent in the business to Coca-Cola for £30 million.

When John Mudd decided to start up a business selling traditional hand-cooked crisps, he conducted some distinctly unorthodox market research by putting Marks & Spencer's crisps, which were similar to the style of crisp he wanted to make, in plain paper bags and asking people in pubs what they thought of them. Not exactly qualitative research, but at least he was in the right place, talking to the right people about what they liked and disliked. When 80 per cent of the pub-goers said they liked the crisps, John went ahead and launched his company, The Real Crisps Company, which went on to be a huge success – partly through sales in pubs.

What do your customers look like?

Never employ an agency to do your market research for you, unless it really is the most basic kind such as counting footfall. It is going to be hard enough to get this thing right without putting hurdles in your way, and if you are trying to interpret what is going on through the conduit of someone else's experiences and impressions you can easily end up with a confusing and murky picture. Ultimately you have to be out there yourself listening, talking and absorbing the mood and acting accordingly.

Armed with the knowledge of who is most likely to buy your product or service, you can then start to compose a mental picture of your target customer, and therefore how you can make your product most appealing to them. Sit down with a blank piece of paper and think about who your customer will be, what age they are, their gender, their lifestyle and family situation, what kind of income they will have, what kind of job they will be doing, how often they will be buying your product and why. Obviously they will not be your only type of customer, but having a clear impression of your main target market will be very helpful.

When Andrew Valentine and Brett Akker started up Streetcar, a car-sharing club in which members can hire cars for anything from half an hour to several days, they realised very early on in their market research that their typical customer was going to be a young professional living in a big city such as London, earning a good salary, who was cash-rich and time-poor and who needed the use of a car but not necessarily the hassle or expense of owning one. So they carefully tailored the service to fill the gap in the market, parking the cars on residential streets where customers could easily access them and providing them with smart cards to make them work. They were also careful to point out in the promotional literature the savings that someone could make by using Streetcar instead of running a car themselves. The research paid off – in 2010 Streetcar had around 50,000 members and was sold to US firm Zipcar for US$50 million (£32.4 million).

ACTION PLAN

▶▶ Draw up a profile of your potential customers. How old are they? What gender? Are they married, do they have children? Where do they live?

▶▶ Now think about how often they are likely to buy from you. Once a day? Once a week? Once a month? Once a year? The answer will make an enormous difference to whether you have a viable business proposition or not.

▶▶ Think about where your customers are likely to spend their time and go and talk to them. Take samples of your product with you and ask for their reaction.

▶▶ The next time you go on holiday, take a look around you. Are there any products or services there that you think might work well back at home? It doesn't really matter where you actually go on holiday: good ideas can come from anywhere. San Francisco might seem to offer more potential than Skegness, but you could be pleasantly surprised.

CHAPTER 5

EMBRACE YOUR INNER DOT COM MILLIONAIRE

It is hard to believe that the internet, in the form of the world wide web, is only twenty years old. It is even more incredible to see how much it has infiltrated and changed our lives. One of the biggest changes, of course, has been to the way we buy things. Every major retail store now runs an online version in parallel with its physical store, and some have gone one better by using the technology to add a whole new dimension. Argos, for example, uses its online shop to improve on the experience of actually going to its stores by enabling people to reserve products online and then go and pick them up in store at their convenience. It's a vast improvement on either trekking to the shop only to find out the product you want is out of stock, or having to wait in all day to have someone deliver it to you.

Even the smallest shops have realised that having their own website and an online presence can substantially increase the flow of customer traffic to their 'real-life' store.

But why have a 'real-life' store at all? Why not simply put your entire business purely online? With the creation of secure online payment systems such as PayPal, and fast broadband connections allowing websites to carry high-quality content such as pictures and videos and advanced search functions, buying via websites has now reached the stage where it is an enjoyable experience. As a result the numbers of customers making transactions online has soared exponentially in the past couple of years. I can now buy virtually everything I could ever need – and, indeed, do – from Amazon, John Lewis and Argos, and each transaction takes me a matter of seconds. In fact, nowadays it is almost too easy. It means that, unfortunately, I buy far more than I ever used to in high street shops, because it is so painless and quick. And if that is what has happened to my buying pattern in the past year or so then it is likely that is what is happening to other people's, too. Which is great news for your business, less so for my bank balance.

All of which means that as a first-time entrepreneur you can, and should, do away with the idea of having a shop or customer-facing premises altogether.

Ditch the shop

There are so many disadvantages to opening a shop, or having an office for customers to visit, and here are just two of them – cost and inflexibility. Opening a shop is a truly expensive business. Apart from the cost of rent – you may also be required to pay an upfront premium – business rates, utilities and signage, you will also have to pay for fitting the shop out and hiring shop assistants unless you plan on spending all day every day there yourself.

Then there is the inflexibility. With a shop you have to stay put while you try to persuade customers to come and see you. The ability to advertise yourself is limited to the people actually walking past the shop and looking in your window, and your opening hours are limited to the times when they might actually be walking past. Not so on the internet.

Getting a good location can be the stuff of nightmares, too. There is a shop near where I live which is the equivalent of a retail black hole. At first glance it looks as if it could be quite a promising site – nice area, close to a good shopping street, near to a large, popular park – but, in fact, on closer inspection, it has a list of negatives a mile long which far outnumber the positives. There is nowhere to leave your car, it is on the wrong side of the street so never gets the sun and is in permanent gloom, and it is stuck on the corner so no one really notices it until they have driven past and it is too late to stop.

Unfortunately, this means that for the past forty years, according to my neighbour who has lived there all his life, the shop has changed hands every six months or so, as each hopeful tenant pitches up with a bagful of cash and a sackful of dreams and then proceeds to lose both in an extremely short space of time. Its most recent reincarnation was as a restaurant and it too was gone in the space of six months. So sad and yet so predictable.

Online onwards and upwards

Contrast that with the benefits of putting your business entirely online. Your costs are limited to setting up a website with an e-commerce function, for which a website designer will charge you around £3,500 to create a good, well-functioning one. Or nothing at all upfront if you decide to bring someone on board to run the website in exchange for equity in the business. Then there is the flexibility. Instead of you standing behind a counter hour after hour, day after day, waiting for your customers to find you, you can be doing something else while your website becomes your virtual shop assistant and tells them everything they need to know. And thanks to search engines such as Google and Yahoo!, you are not just dependent on the number of people physically walking past your shop. With a website you can attract custom from all over the country, and all over the world.

Even better, you can run your business from anywhere in the world, too. That is incredibly useful for people living in rural areas where the local population is not large enough to support a bricks and mortar business, and where transport links are poor. Whereas once those two factors would have been enough to stop someone even considering starting up a business in a rural area, now, with an online business, they simply don't matter at all. All you need is a fast broadband connection and you are up and away. Michael Parker, for example, founder of A Quarter Of, the online sweetshop, left the UK in 2010 with his wife and children and relocated permanently to Spain, to a beautiful and very remote Andalusian village, after realising that, as his business was run entirely online, he could just as easily manage it from there as he could from the UK.

And the best thing of all is that these days you can sell virtually anything online – and, what's more, customers expect to be able to buy anything that way. Deirdre Bounds, for example, made a lot of money running TEFL (teaching English as a foreign language) courses online, something which at first glance one would have thought impossible. She went on to create, and then sell for a large sum, i-to-i, a business which provides paid volunteer holidays overseas.

Jamie Murray Wells has embraced this idea brilliantly. In 2004 he started selling prescription glasses online, via his website glassesdirect.co.uk. Everyone told him it wouldn't work and that no one would be interested in buying prescription glasses over the internet rather than buying them from an optician. But Jamie didn't listen to the gloom-mongers. He went ahead anyway, selling his glasses at just £15 a pair, a fraction of the cost that opticians charged, something he was able to do because he did not have the huge overhead costs of maintaining a chain of shops. Sales took off so Jamie started selling contact lenses online too, and his annual turnover is now more than £10 million.

And now Jamie has embarked on an even bolder venture – selling hearing aids online, through a new website called hearingdirect.com. It is the ideal product to sell online because it is so light and easy to post. But what is really clever about this is that Jamie has used the possibilities of the internet itself to enable him to do this – customers can actually check their hearing online through the site first, so they know which hearing aid they should be buying.

It's not the same, it's better

The amazing thing about putting a business online is that you can come up with all sorts of business ideas that would never have existed and don't even really work in the real physical shop world. Daniel Laurence has created an incredibly successful business out of selling stickers which teachers award to pupils who have done well. But that is just the beginning of it. His online business schoolstickers.co.uk allows schools to personalise the stickers they send home with the school's name and the subject. It even prints a unique number on each merit sticker which pupils can record on a separate but linked website – mystickers.co.uk – and so collect points that can be redeemed for prizes. Teachers, meanwhile, have their own third, linked website where they can input the names of pupils and find out what merits they have been given. On top of all this, Daniel has created a virtual online world at vizwoz.com where children can spend their points on virtual prizes. To make it as safe as possible for young pupils to use, he bought up all possible connotations of the domain name, including spelling mistakes, and the site is monitored twenty-four hours a day. All of this is utterly baffling to anyone over the age of thirty but the business now has a turnover of around £4 million.

As both Jamie Murray Wells and Daniel Laurence have discovered, creating a business online is about far more than simply relocating a physical business into cyberspace. The internet opens up all kinds of possibilities to do business differently and better, in ways that are just not possible with a physical shop. To take a very basic example, many online guitar shops actually play the notes corresponding to the strings of a guitar, so that you can tune your guitar without having to turn the house upside down in search of a tuning fork. And the website at A Suit That Fits, which makes and sells suits via the internet, enables you not only to design and customise a three-piece suit entirely online, down to the number of buttons and pocket style, it also enables you to measure yourself too, guiding you through the process with video clips and images.

Just look what you can do

Putting your business online also enables you to build a virtual community of your customers, which would be impossible in real life. By encouraging people to register their details when buying you can create a virtual club where customers can receive news and updates and get discounts on future products. You can personalise it further, as Jamie Murray Wells and his team do, by writing a regular blog, or online diary, on the site.

Customers can also, of course, write reviews of your products, either on your website, if you enable it, or on others. Through price comparison websites they can also compare the price of your product with your competitors'. Websites like mumsnet.com and babycentre.co.uk, for example, have a forum where users can review baby products by every manufacturer. And, as we are seeing, customers are becoming increasingly vocal and increasingly happy to share their experiences with others on the web.

In fact, this is really the biggest leap in taking your business online – your business is far more transparent and open to scrutiny than it would be hiding away in a corner shop somewhere. This is either a fantastically good thing or a fantastically bad thing, of course, depending on how good your business is.

The most exciting thing from your point of view as a fledgling entrepreneur is that this openness and transparency is not a one-way street. Putting your business online means that you can find out a lot more about your customers than you could running a high street shop. Website analysis tools such as Google Analytics can help you find out where your customers are coming from – whether they are arriving by word of mouth, via the search engines or from direct links through an advertising campaign, for example. They can also tell you how many people are visiting your site and help you identify what is deterring potential customers, by showing you data such as the bounce rate, which indicates when people enter your site and then leave right away, and the abandonment rate, which shows when they start filling the shopping basket and then leave. It may show that visitors to your site get lost on page two of the sales transaction process, for example, which lets you know that you need to redesign it.

Simply rewriting the tags and straplines on your home page can also turn visitors into paying customers – it may be that you are driving people away by asking for their date of birth or other information you don't really need, for example. It is crucial to make your customers' journey from arriving at the site to actually buying something as easy and painless as possible.

The other huge advantage of having your business entirely online, of course, is that suddenly you are no longer limited by geographical boundaries. Your website can be seen and visited by anyone anywhere in the world, which means that you can potentially sell to anyone anywhere in the world, provided you can work out how to deliver your product or service. In order to make this potential a reality, you really need to have a website address that ends in .com (make sure you get .co.uk too if you are based in the UK and arrange it so that one clicks through automatically to the other).

But you have to stand out from the crowd

A word of warning: if you are going to launch an online business then you must make sure that you really do have something original and different to offer. The internet is now so crowded with fledgling businesses that simply creating an online version of a business that has been trad-itionally done from a shop or office is just not good enough. I have lost count of the number of online recruitment agen-cies that have sprung up, each with ever more wacky names but each still offering essentially the same thing. Not only are they all competing with each other, they are all competing with the biggest players in the industry which operate both online and on the high street.

And if you are going to put your business entirely online, you do need to put some effort into making it look good, and work well. Anything that looks amateur or confusing, or, worse, anything that doesn't work properly is not going to last long. Customers will come and look once and then never again. And they will tell their friends not to bother either.

At the very least your website should be straightforwardly laid out and easy to read – no white writing on black background, please, and nothing too small – with good, useful pictures. Don't make the mistake that lots of websites make by crowding too much on to the front page. And don't make it so high-tech that it requires the very latest in computer technology to run correctly. And don't use flashing banners unless you want customers to run away screaming. Remember, you are trying to encourage them to stay, not give them a blinding headache. It should also be easy to navigate so that customers can find their way around it without getting lost. The online shop section of it should be logical and easy to use, with functions to retain customer information for future shopping and instant email confirmations and ongoing delivery information.

Get people to test it out too, and be prepared to change it if you realise that something jars. Will Sussman, who lives on the Isle of Wight, saw bookings rise almost overnight when he revamped the website for his chalet holiday company meribelskichalets.co.uk. He says: 'I made silly mistakes on the original website, such as white print on a blue background. We changed it to black on white, made it all much clearer, got a new logo and spent money on nice images.' His revamp worked. He says: 'In less than a week I had phone calls from customers saying they were booking because they loved the website.'

Consider the role of your website designer

If you are in any way computer literate it can be tempting to design your website yourself. You should certainly make all the final decisions about what it actually looks like, but, remember, you have an awful lot of other things on your plate. And don't rely on a helpful friend or family member to create your website as a favour either, unless they really do know what they are doing. This is one area in which you really do need to get professional help in the form of a competent website designer. Make sure that it is coded onto a good content management system such as WordPress and then you can easily make small changes to the content yourself without having to rely on the designer to do it every time. But if you think that upgrading and improving your website and adding greater functionality is likely to be of ongoing importance to your business – and it may well be, given that your website is going to be your sole window to the world – then when you find a website designer you like and get on with, I suggest you try to make them a permanent part of your business by establishing a long-term relationship with them.

If you look at Facebook, or Amazon, or even Marks & Spencer and Tesco, they are continually adding new features to their websites and improving their functionality. The very nature of websites is that new things are being made possible all the time, and something that may not have been possible to do six months ago may be possible now, and you need to have someone on board who can both tell you about it and do it.

Your website expert can also take over the vital job of making sure that your website has the best possible chance of actually being found by potential customers, by using search engine optimisation to make sure that when, for example, people type 'gardening tools in Croydon' into a search engine such as Google, your business pops up on the first page of the results. Again, it can be tempting to think you can do all this yourself, too, but even if you can, you shouldn't. Once you start getting into the complex world of search engine optimisation – which at its most basic involves putting key words in the content of your website and making sure that Google picks them up, but quickly gets a lot more complicated – then entire days can pass as you get more and more involved in it. Days you should be spending setting up and running your business and doing all the mundane stuff like opening a business bank account and registering your business for VAT.

If the idea of starting up your business entirely online instead of on the ground makes you sad because you had really been looking forward to the idea of getting to know your customers in person, it is possible to build that in too, at least before your business gets too big.

That is what Sarah Manby has done. She started up her online business Mango Mutt selling natural and organic accessories for dogs in 2004 after finding it impossible to find a nice collar for her black Labrador, Murphy.

Being passionate about dogs, she realised she did not want Mango Mutt to be simply another anonymous website selling products, but wanted to get to know her customers person-ally as well. So she started replying individually to every customer's email, asking them how their dogs were getting on. She also started up a forum for dog owners on the site and regularly walks her dog with local customers and their dogs.

She says: 'Buying something online can be a very soulless experience. You are sat at a computer and you just get an automated response that your goods have been dispatched. I believe that the way forward for a small business such as Mango Mutt is by getting to know your customers and that will then hopefully make them want to come back and purchase from me again. When you have a dog, you already have a connection.'

When she set up a forum on the website asking customers for their feedback the response was overwhelmingly positive. She says: 'Customers were telling me they love the experience of shopping with Mango Mutt because they feel a part of the business and that is what makes them want to come back. I never want to stop treating my customers like individuals because I think that is what has made my small business succeed in the last couple of years.'

ACTION PLAN

▶▶ Draw up a list of e-commerce business websites you like and work out why you like them – is it their visual design, or their ease of use, or their use of photos, for example? Then design your website around the features you like. But don't stray too far from the accepted style of how a website should look – you want your customers to feel immediately comfortable on entering your site, not completely baffled as to how it works.

▶▶ Find yourself a website designer. Go on personal recommendation, ask to see previous work first and ask for references and phone numbers of previous clients – then talk to them to find out how pleasant, or otherwise, the experience was. Yes, it really is that important.

▶▶ Get lots of people to try out your site in its pre-launch version and tell you what the experience was like. Not just friends but people who will be brutally honest.

CHAPTER 6

LAUGH IN THE FACE OF BANK LOANS

When Niall Holden decided to start his own equipment hire business in 1987 at the age of twenty-six, he managed to persuade NatWest to give him a start-up loan of £5,000. He promptly booked a holiday in Rhodes for himself and his business partner and the two of them spent the next three weeks lying on a beach. Then, when they got home, they each bought themselves a company car. By now they were down to their last £128, with little to show for their efforts but a nice tan. At which point they finally decided to get to work and start their business, VDC Trading, renting out microphone stands and cables. Niall has had the last laugh, too – from that £128 he has managed to create a business with an annual turnover of £6 million.

These days, sadly, banks are no longer quite so carefree

with their money and if you are trying to start up a business for the first time with no previous experience, you are likely to get short shrift from your local bank manager.

Even if you are able to get a loan, nowadays that can bring with it as many headaches as being turned down for one. First off, the raft of fees that come attached to a loan – arrangement fees, administration fees, renewal fees – on top of the interest rate is likely to make the cost of borrowing the money very expensive. In practical terms it means that every month the first chunk of money you make goes instantly to the bank. Before you have even sold a thing you have a huge debt burden hanging around your neck.

Then there is the fact that in order to get the loan in the first place it is very likely that you will have had to put up your home as security for the loan. Not a nice feeling when the business is having a bad month and the prospect of becoming homeless as well as business-less looms large in your nightmares.

Finally, there is the very real worry that if you miss a monthly payment the banks will swoop in on you and demand their money back immediately, in full. In short, borrowing large amounts to fund your business launch is stressful and expensive and it allows very little margin for error.

It is not much less stressful borrowing from your friends or family either. Yes, they are likely to be more forgiving if you miss the odd payment or two, and they are unlikely to demand your home as security or start trying to charge you arrangement fees. But think for a moment about the conse- quences if, for whatever reason, your business failed and you lost all their money. It would be truly, truly awful. You wouldn't be able to pay them back and the anger, the guilt, the unspoken blame and the embarrassment would over-shadow and sour every subsequent family gathering or friends' night out for a very long time to come.

There is a solution

The obvious answer is to start up a business that does not require a chunky bank loan or overdraft to get it going. The good news is that it is entirely possible to start up a successful business with little or no money – and, even better, the amount of money you start with has absolutely no bearing on the amount of money you could eventually make. Remember all those dot com companies which burned through hundreds of thousands of pounds of start-up cash and then promptly sank without trace? On the other hand, I know of dozens of successful entrepreneurs who started with virtually no money at all and have gone on to create amazing businesses.

Or how about this approach? If your business needs money that you haven't got, then you may be able to get round the problem simply by being inventive. Karen Earl managed to start her eponymous sports sponsorship agency with no money at all after one of her first clients agreed to pay their entire first year's fee in advance. She went on to sell the business for £4 million.

Get stuff for free

Another way of getting by without needing a bank loan or overdraft is to get things for free that you would normally expect to pay for. Many IT services, for example, can be found free online, from invoicing and project management tools to online storage and office software. Google's Analytics, Insight and Trends tools enable instant and free market research, while social networking sites such as Twitter, Facebook, online forums and chat rooms allow you to get in touch with potential customers for nothing. As a start-up you can also enjoy the benefits of a trend in which online service providers increasingly offer basic services free and charge only for premium services.

There's no need to spend much on kitting out your home office with furniture either. You may be able to find what you are looking for on websites such as freecycle.org and gumtree.com, which list free office furniture and equipment. Or, of course, there is always that time-honoured classic beloved of fledgling entrepreneurs – the kitchen table.

There are other ways of cutting start-up costs, too. Take advertising. Many small businesses waste huge sums of money on advertising because they think that it is something they should be doing, without giving it any more thought. They take a small advert in the back of a glossy magazine at a cost of perhaps £3,000 and then they sit back and hope for the best. Unfortunately, with so many adverts competing for readers' attention, it is likely to be money down the drain. The cheaper and more effective solution is to spend time on doing your own public relations instead. If you are prepared to think creatively, there are many ways of bringing your product or service to the public's attention for free or for little cost. Offer some of your products as prizes for a competition in your local newspaper, sponsor a float in your town's summer carnival. Little cost to you, great coverage, great local recognition.

Consider equity stakes for vital helpers

One option many start-ups planning an online business take is to give the person designing their website an equity stake instead of paying them. This is not a good idea if the job is likely to be simply a one-off website design and launch, the bulk of which will be done within the space of a few months, but if you are looking for someone to play an active and busy role continually updating and servicing and expanding the website then having the IT as part of the company could work very well indeed. And not just financially but for the long-term commitment that it brings. Darren Richards, who founded the original British dating website Dating Direct, for example, gave a 20 per cent stake in the business to his website designer when he started up the company. Everyone told him he was mad to do it but Darren says he has never regretted the decision because it put the website and the management of it at the very heart of the business, which for something like a dating website was very much where it needed to be. Having started the business up with just £2,500, Darren sold it a few years ago for £30 million.

Or how about a bit of bartering?

Another way forward for start-ups to avoid taking on debt is by bartering, whereby businesses swap services with each other rather than paying for them. The exciting thing about bartering is that it can not only save you money, it can also lead to other benefits. First, offering something in kind tends to create a greater bond than if cash were simply changing hands. Second, by paying in kind rather than cash, each side is offering a product or service that is worth cost price to them, but retail price to the other side – to the benefit of both.

Peter Spencer, the founder of Le Bureau, which provides shared work space in Battersea, south London, was initially strongly opposed to the idea of bartering. But when a computer expert offered to revamp his IT system in return for free desk space for four months, Peter agreed to give it a go. He is now a convert and has tried bartering several more times, including giving office space to a marketing person and a graphic designer who designed Peter's website and all his logos in return for desk space.

He says: 'Bartering is good because you feel like you are helping someone, and it establishes an emotional bond because there is no exchange of money. It makes you feel more appreciated. It is a friendlier way of doing business but it is more than that because you get more bang for your buck. In each case I found that we were both prepared to offer more so both of us had a better experience because of it.'

Amanda Farren, meanwhile, organises baby fairs at which small businesses take stands to exhibit their products. She was recently happy to swap a stand at the baby fair she was organising in Coventry for a term of swimming lessons for her daughter. A great deal for her – and a great deal for the small firm taking the stand. The swap came about when Amanda contacted the owner of a local business which ran swimming classes to arrange lessons for her daughter and happened to mention the baby fair to her. The two agreed to do a swap – but, more than that, they have stayed in touch and established a business relationship that could work well for both of them in the future.

Start-ups may even be able to get PR in return for bartering their products. Jo Sensini is the owner of Velvet Integrated PR, based in west London. She recently agreed to be paid £1,000 in chocolate for some work and had also agreed to be paid in shoes by another client for a project that never went ahead.

Get your customers to pay upfront

Perhaps the most exciting and lasting solution to the question of how to avoid borrowing money is to start up a business which doesn't actually need money – because the customers pay you before you have to pay your suppliers. In other words, a business which is always cash positive. Other side benefits include no bad debts, and no time spent chasing them – because if customers don't pay, they don't get the product or service. Simple as that. Such an idea may sound too good to be true but a number of small businesses have discovered that it can and does work – brilliantly.

Sylvia Tidy-Harris started up her public-speaking agency The Speakers Agency in 2001 with £1,000 in cash. She has never had to take out a loan or ask for an overdraft facility and she never has sleepless nights about whether a client is going to pay their bill or where she will find the money to pay a speaker. The reason for this is simple – she gets the money upfront from clients wishing to book a speaker which she puts into a client holding account and only pays the speaker once they have delivered a speech, which can be several months later. As a result her business is always, and has always been, in credit, and she has never suffered any bad debts. Now the business has seven hundred speakers on its books and an annual turnover of £1 million.

Sylvia says: 'I just wanted a straightforward business that would work. Nobody ever told me to take the money upfront but I just thought it was logical because you can't take back a speech; it is not like selling furniture which you can take back. There are enough concerns in business without having to worry about repaying a loan.'

She says that in all the years she has been in business only four clients have ever been upset about the idea of paying her upfront. The reason so few people object, says Sylvia, is because they know they will get their money back if the speaker does not fulfil his or her side of the deal.

Sylvia helps to ensure the company always stays in credit by keeping fixed costs as low as possible. No swanky London office for her and her five staff – they rent a small office in Ibstock, Leicestershire, next door to a bookmakers and a chip shop, for £500 a month.

She says: 'I have never had to worry about how we are going to pay the bills and that in business is the biggest relief of all.'

Claire Brynteson also runs a business which has never needed a loan or overdraft. At her business, Buy Time, which provides temporary PAs and concierge services by the hour, customers pay upfront for blocks of time and she pays her workers in arrears at the end of each month.

Claire, who started up her business in 2003 with £20,000,

part of her redundancy money from her previous job, says she modelled her business on the idea of pay-as-you-go mobile phones, liking the ease and simplicity of the way in which people could buy phone credit upfront and then use it whenever they wanted. She has never had a bank loan and has had negligible bad debts.

She says: 'I set up the business this way to minimise the risk of cash-flow problems. I probably sleep a lot better at night than many other small business owners at the moment because unlike them I don't feel stressed about money. I would hate to think that a bank could demand their money back, simply because of external circumstances which might have nothing to do with my business. I am glad I don't have that pressure on me. By running my business this way I have complete control and complete confidence that my business is not going to be affected by changing attitudes of banks to small firms.'

The payment upfront model can even work for businesses in market sectors which do not traditionally charge this way.

David Sandy is the owner of Integreat Media, which designs websites for small and medium-sized businesses. He started it up in 2006 with £1,000 of personal savings and now runs it in his spare time from his home in Winkfield Row, near Bracknell in east Berkshire. In his day job he is a web developer for the NHS.

Whenever he is taken on to design a website, he asks the client for 50 per cent of the cost upfront, and then gets the balance before the website he has designed goes live. He says: 'In effect I am getting the entire 100 per cent payment upfront before the total product is available to their clients.'

The upside for him is obvious. The upside for his clients, he says, is that they are able to secure his services for the duration of the entire project. Even better, he says that taking payment in this way establishes a real bond of mutual trust between him and the client from the start.

He says: 'I have never had anyone refuse to pay the deposit. Generally they are very happy.'

He has never had any bad debts. If a small firm really cannot afford to pay the 50 per cent upfront, David may agree on a smaller deposit, but only after he has satisfied himself through his own personal research that the firm looks sound.

He adds: 'I speak regularly to other businesses who do have debts with banks and it certainly is an added pressure on them. I am relieved and I am lucky that my business does not have to be in that situation.'

David also offers full-year support contracts for website development for large organisations and even manages to get some of them to pay him upfront, twelve months in advance.

So if you think your business model could be shaped into this way of working, it might be worth looking closely at it. No, it is not usual, or traditional, and obviously it will generally not work for something like manufacturing where business customers need to inspect your products for quality assurance. And if you are selling to big businesses, as opposed to retail customers, they are likely to insist that you work to their terms and conditions rather than the other way round. But if you have a product or service that people really want, then making them pay upfront for it could be the best business decision you ever made.

ACTION PLAN

▶▶ Write a list of all your planned start-up costs, in other words the money you are going to need to start up your business. Now look at every item on your list in turn and try to find a way of eliminating it. Can you lease instead of buying? Can you get something for free instead of paying for it? Do you really need an office, or a company car, or the services of a public relations agency at this point? Or can they wait until the business can pay for them itself?

▶▶ Now write down a list of your proposed customers. Is there some way of persuading them to pay upfront – or sooner – for your products or services, perhaps by discounting the price for early payment?

▶▶ Start being creative. Think about how you might be able to swap your products or services for something else you would otherwise have had to pay for.

CHAPTER 7

BE SINGLE-MINDED

I have a very good friend called Will Wolseley who comes from Somerset but who, in 1992, decided to grow a vineyard from scratch in Australia. He spent a long time looking for the land he needed and he finally found it in the hills above the surfing town of Torquay in the state of Victoria. It was a patch of land which had never had vines growing on it, and it was situated in an area not known for its wine-making. But Will thought it might have potential because it was close to the ocean and had a maritime climate. So, even though everyone told him he was mad, he went ahead and bought the land for AU$80,000, then equivalent to £29,000. Because he had spent all his savings buying the land, he cleared it himself by hand and then painstakingly planted every single vine himself, also by hand, all 11,250 of them. He tended them all carefully and watched them grow and, six years later, they rewarded him for his care and attention when they produced grapes perfect for turning into wine. And he then started making fantastic wines out of them.

But the really interesting part of this story is that, in contrast to the care and attention Will lavished on his vines day after day, for himself he spent just half a day erecting a makeshift tent from wooden posts and green plastic sheeting, with a galvanised iron sheet for a roof. His bed was a mattress on the floor and the kitchen comprised a single cold-water pipe. If you happened to drive past his house by chance you would have thought it was a temporary shack for storing things in. At best.

In fact, until recently that would still have been the case, because Will was so obsessed with making the best wine he could that he ended up living in that makeshift shack for fifteen years. Every time he made a bit of money from selling his wines, he would reinvest every penny of it in building storage for the wines, rather than accommodation for himself, and then building a proper winery. And even when he did finally move out of his shack, it was only to move into a prefabricated cabin he has erected on the site. It has a window and a proper floor, but there are few mod cons and the toilet is what Will euphemistically describes as an 'organic long drop'.

His wine, meanwhile, has flourished. It is highly regarded by wine critics and customers alike and has won lots of awards – you can check it out at wolseleywines.com. Will now produces around 40,000 bottles a year, supplies some of the best restaurants in Australia and has been hailed as a pioneer of winemaking in his region.

And the plastic-sided tent is, I think, the secret of his

success. Will has been so utterly single-minded about what he was doing that he has always focused on what was important to the business – and completely ignored everything that was not. He sends out madly enthusiastic emails about his wine and eighteen years on is clearly still in love with the whole process. Now forty-four, he is still so besotted with his wine that, given half the chance, he will talk long into the night about grape varieties and soils. As he writes with some understatement on his website, 'We focus exclusively on winemaking, not grandstanding.'

Being single-minded is an occupational hazard for an entrepreneur – and also the key to becoming a successful one. It is a simple question of maths. Given that there are only twenty-four hours in a day and seven days in a week, you need to focus on the things that matter to you in order to get anything done.

Philip Weldon freely admits he paid a high price for becoming an entrepreneur. He is the founder of The English Cheesecake Company, which now has a turnover of £3 million a year, but for the first ten years of making cheesecakes he never had a girlfriend and hardly ever socialised with friends. He says: 'I was so single-minded that everything else was shut out. It wasn't possible to even think about anybody or anything other than the business.'

Happily, Philip has since made up for lost time and at the age of fifty he now has a girlfriend and a baby. But he makes a very real and valid point – that in order to get a business off the ground and flourishing you really do need to be single-minded in the early days to have any chance of making it work.

Don't get sidetracked

It is also important not to get sidetracked by other projects and, for an enthusiastic first-time entrepreneur who is fizzing and buzzing with new ideas, this can be the hardest one of all to put into practice. What if the idea you are pursuing is not really THE BIG ONE? What if this other idea you have could have the potential to be the big one, if only you had the time and energy to devote more resources to it? Should you abandon one in order to pursue the other? And what happens if you make the wrong choice? Or should you be trying to do both projects A and B at the same time and hope that it quickly becomes obvious which one is going to be the big success and which one isn't?

This was the dilemma facing Will King, who had started up his shaving oil business, King of Shaves, but then had a moment of doubt one year into the project after the business racked up losses of £30,000 and everyone close to him told him it would be a failure. He says: 'I had this tiny little bottle of oil and nobody believed it would work. When I told people I was going to go up against Gillette and change the face of shaving, they would yawn and say, how are you going to do that?'

Indeed, everyone else was so doubtful about his chances of success that King thought he ought to have a Plan B. So he started up a sideline business selling surf clothing called Bodyglove, which had featured on the television series *Baywatch*. It was a stupendously bad idea. The new business took up a lot of his time and it soon became clear that it was by no means obvious that this venture would work either.

He recalls: 'It was a nightmare. Everybody thought the clothing business would work really well but none of the surf shops paid their bills and it was hugely time-intensive.' After two years of trying to do both his shaving oil business and his surf clothing business, he closed the latter down. He says: 'Then I realised I had nearly mucked up King of Shaves because I was juggling too many balls.'

Starting up a business is a bit like buying a house. Once you have bought it, you really do have to stop looking at property websites and at all the other houses you could have bought instead. Because if you don't you will start seeing all the faults in the house you did buy and begin to wonder if you made the right decision, and you will start to drive yourself mad.

So here's what to do. If you are starting a business and you are not sure if it is going to work, then commit to it fully for the first year, say, and then reassess the situation. You simply can't pursue two business ideas at the same time with the same intensity, not least because by pursuing two of them you are in effect admitting to yourself that the first one may not work. And if you don't believe it is going to work, then why should anyone else? So choose which to do first and do it wholeheartedly.

It still might fail, of course, but being half-hearted about something is effectively condemning it to failure before it has even had a proper chance to get going. Not only that, but if you have two fledgling businesses on the go at the same time then other people – customers, suppliers, investors – will quickly spot your lack of commitment, too.

One of the first questions the Dragons on *Dragons' Den* invariably ask of the people seeking investment is what else they have going on in their lives; they always look appalled if they discover the person has other projects bubbling away. With good reason. Your business needs to be the thing you dream about every night and wake up thinking about every morning. Do one at a time and do it well.

Stick to what you are good at

It can be frighteningly easy to take your eye off the ball even when you have only one business to think about. Paul Gregg and his wife Nita had built up a successful business running theatres across the country, including the Apollo Victoria in London, the New Theatre in Oxford and the Bristol Hippodrome. But one day they decided to try producing a show themselves. After seeing Richard Harris play King Arthur in *Camelot* on Broadway, they brought the play to London. Paul says: 'When we saw the show in New York, I went to sleep in the first half with jet lag but I came back to London absolutely convinced that Richard Harris in *Camelot* was a good idea. So we put it on and had fantastic previews – and then got the most dreadful reviews. Suddenly what was a record-breaking business in the West End turned into the worst business in the world.'

The show ran for only eight weeks and Paul ended up losing £750,000. He says now: 'It was a big lesson. I realised that making money out of producing shows is a specialist business and you have to be single-minded about it. The truth is we should have stayed being theatre owners.'

Paul went back to what he knew best, running theatres, and then hit the big time with the arrival of Andrew Lloyd Webber's *Starlight Express* at his Apollo Victoria, where it ran for seventeen years. Paul eventually sold his theatre business for £120 million.

The fact is that being single-minded about your business can really help to get things done, and to cut out all unnecessary noise. When David Levin decided to develop his first hotel in London, a small boutique hotel near Harrods in Knightsbridge, he was so focused on getting it done right and on time that when a steel strike halted construction, he went to Germany himself in a lorry to buy steel after getting his architects to convert their plans into metric.

He finally opened The Capital Hotel for business in 1971 with ten rooms and a restaurant. When no customers turned up he took matters into his own hands and wrote to the restaurant critic of the *Evening Standard*, the London evening newspaper, and invited him to visit. Fortunately, the critic loved it. The next night the restaurant was full and bookings for the hotel soon followed.

The Capital Hotel now has a five-star rating and is a member of the Small Luxury Hotels of the World group. It is regularly named Best Small Hotel of the Year in the annual London Tourism Awards.

Mark Ellingham, who founded the Rough Guides, is another successful entrepreneur who puts his achievements down to being extremely single-minded. His publishing empire, which now includes two hundred titles, started with a single book, *The Rough Guide to Greece*, which Mark wrote when he graduated from university and couldn't find a job. He went to Greece for a couple of months to work out what to do with his life, and while he was there he realised there might be a gap in the market for a guidebook that combined practical advice with a real insight into the country's culture. So he wrote a couple of chapters and when he returned home managed to find a small publisher who agreed to pay him an advance of £900 to finish it.

The book was a huge success – within weeks of publication it was reprinted twice – and so Mark agreed to write a series of Rough Guides. When the original publisher was taken over by another company, Mark bought the imprint himself and the guides have since sold more than twenty million copies. In 2004 Mark and his two partners sold 51 per cent of the company to Penguin for £5 million and then in 2008 sold the other 49 per cent for a further £5 million.

He says: 'I can see an idea and run with it and not be afraid to try it and put money into it. If you believe you can do something better or different, you shouldn't be intimidated. You have to plough your own furrow.'

Make time for your family

Unfortunately, there is a downside to all this single-mindedness. For some people being so completely focused on making your business work can also make you forget about the people close to you – your family and partner and children. Look at the personal history of any successful entrepreneur and the chances are that they will be on to their second or even third marriage. Rik Hellewell, who founded oven-cleaning service Ovenu, thinks that his single-minded determination to make the business work and his long working hours contributed to the breakdown of his first marriage.

He says: 'Anybody can be successful at whatever it is they want to do if they want to do it enough. But you have to be prepared to put in the extra hours and be blinkered. You are not born lucky, you make your own luck. If you are going to do something, you have to do it wholeheartedly with the ultimate objective of winning the race. Nobody ever remembers the person who came second.'

If you are using family savings to start up your business then the potential for rift and discord is even greater, particularly if your using it means that other family things, such as going on holiday or buying a new car or moving house, have to be put on hold. Although your family may end up sharing in some of the rewards if and when your business is a success, that could be many years hence. And in any case it can be hard for them to believe in the promise of future fortunes when the business looks as though it could be about to consume every last penny of the family savings.

The times when the rift between work and family can become particularly acute are during festive occasions such as Christmas and over the summer holidays. If you continually make phone calls and check your emails while you are on the beach making sandcastles with your children, or you are glued to your laptop while the kids are opening presents and having fun, then it is easy to see how your fledgling business can become your family's equivalent of the bogeyman. And it can be just as annoying the other way round, when you need to make an important phone call and your kids suddenly choose that exact moment to start yelling at each other.

If you want to prevent your family ganging up on you, then when you are with them switch off completely from work for a few hours and spend real quality time with them. Don't try to half-do both, such as surreptitiously checking your emails when you think no one is looking, because they will quickly cotton on to what you are up to and you will just infuriate everyone – including yourself, as you won't be able to concentrate properly anyway.

One solution to this is to get your family involved so that they really do feel part of the business and can share in your successes. That way there is immediately less confrontation between your business and your family and there is less need to choose one at the expense of the other. What's more, when they are involved in the business and can see it from the inside looking out, and realise just what commitment it requires from you to make it a success, they are more likely to feel less alienated and more able to support you.

I have lost count of the number of successful entrepreneurs who now formally involve their husbands/wives/partners/ children in the business. Don Lewin, the founder of Clinton Cards, has brought both his son and his daughter into the business, while both Emma Bridgewater, who makes painted pottery, and Justine Cather, whose business Burnt Sugar makes old-fashioned fudge and sweets, brought their husbands into the businesses a few years after starting them up.

Twin brothers Jim and Geoff Riley have gone one better and in 2002 started up their business, Tutor2u.net, together. The business provides educational resources for teachers and revision workshops for students.

Jim says they initially started up the business together as a way of developing a closer bond when their father was diagnosed with terminal cancer. He says: 'We decided that we would like to build something together as a way of keeping in touch. Before this we would, like many brothers do, talk relatively infrequently; it would be family holidays and the occasional meet-up. But this business has given us a reason to talk every day. That was the most important thing.'

But being related has been beneficial for the business, too. Jim says: 'Because we are twins we share the same instincts and the same concept of what we are trying to do. It means that the communication barriers between us are almost non-existent and because of that decision-making is so much easier and quicker.' Their working method clearly works – Tutor2u.net, which they set up by investing £1,000 each, is now worth around £3 million.

ACTION PLAN

▶▶ **Practise efficient working to make the most of the time available to you. If you have an hour to do some work, then sit down and do the work and don't get up until the hour is gone. Don't keep breaking off to check emails, to make a cup of tea, to open the post, to check the cricket score.**

▶▶ **Make a list in descending order of what is most important to you right now, and what can be postponed for five years. Starting a business, moving house, going on long holidays, having an active social life. Be realistic. You are unlikely to be able to have it all, so decide what you need to have now and what can wait.**

▶▶ **Call a family meeting – or a meeting of your close friends, or both – and explain to them what you are doing and why. Try to get their support, or, failing that, at least help them understand why you are doing this. Think of ways in which they might want to get involved.**

CHAPTER 8

GET TO GRIPS WITH THE IDEA OF RISK

Not long ago I received an email from a *Sunday Times* reader asking for my advice. After telling me he had recently been made redundant from his job of seventeen years, he explained that he had come up with an innovative idea for an accessory for a kitchen appliance. He said that the feedback he had received so far had been extremely encouraging so he had employed a product design company to come up with some designs based on his drawings.

Then he went on to tell me that he had a wife and child who depended on him financially and that he had had to sell his car to pay for the designs he was having done. He hoped that the designs on their own would be enough to pitch to potential buyers without his needing to get an actual prototype of his product made. And that a big buyer would

place an order as a result of seeing the designs, which would
be enough to pay for the cost of getting the product made.

He said that he hoped to sell his product to major DIY
stores and catalogue shops, adding: 'I am convinced my idea
will work, I am just trying to establish a way into the marketplace. I plan to have my product on the shelves by the end
of this year.' (It was the end of July when he emailed me.)
He ended his email asking if I could put him in touch with
'any heads of procurement within the field' and thanking
me in advance for any help I would be able to offer him
with his project.

Well, I don't know what your answer to this email would
have been, but I can tell you what mine was. I wrote back
instantly saying PLEASE DON'T DO IT. There were so many
parts of his email that shouted out that this was an incredibly bad idea and a financial disaster waiting to happen. The
idea of trying to invent a new product without any money
other than the proceeds from selling his car, and having no
knowledge of whether there would even be any demand for
his product. Thinking that he would be able to get an order
from someone based only on graphic designs of the product
rather than on an actual prototype (how would they be able
to test that it actually worked and met safety and quality
standards?). And thinking that the whole thing could be
finished and on the shelves within a matter of months. And,
in the meantime, him having no money and no job and
having to support two people who relied on him. I just
couldn't see how any of it could possibly work. Frankly, the
whole idea sent a shiver of alarm down my spine. I emailed
him back suggesting in the strongest possible way that he

find a less risky business to start up, if that was what he really wanted to do, such as selling a proven product into a proven market, or providing a service which would not need such a big initial investment.

Work out what your risk is

There is calculated risk and then there is sheer foolhardiness. When you are starting up a business for the first time you need to be very clear about which path you are taking. It is important to understand that starting a business always involves taking some kind of risk – in the world of business and commerce you need to have risk in order to reap rewards. But there are different levels of risk and different kinds of risk, and you need to find a level you are comfortable with before you proceed.

For some people that level of acceptable risk might entail being prepared to lose a certain amount of money. For others acceptable risk might be the possibility of losing out career-wise if the business doesn't take off and then finding it difficult to get back on to the career path they left. Or it might be the possibility of having to sell your flat and move back home with your parents. Or it might even be the risk of putting a strain on your marriage, or making the children unsettled. Whatever it is, you need to be very clear about what you stand to lose if it all goes wrong, not just what you stand to gain if it all goes right. Blithely answering 'everything' to both questions is not good enough; you need to think this through properly.

The worst thing you can do, as the writer of the email

was doing, is throw everything up in the air and simply hope for the best. Fortune may favour the brave but it does not favour the foolish, and simply putting everything you own on the line does not make it more likely that you will succeed. It merely makes it more likely that, when you fail, it will be a lot more painful.

Just as everyone has a different view about whether they would go bungee-jumping or not – and that's a very big 'no, thank you' from me – so everyone has a different attitude towards risk. So it is important that you try to work out how you really feel about it.

When Tom Dudderidge decided he wanted to start his own business, he initially tried to do the impossible – to find a business idea that carried no risk. He says: 'I was going about it in the wrong way. I would try desperately to have an idea and then when I had an idea I would try desperately to prove that it would definitely succeed. And always in that process I would manage to convince myself that it wasn't worth doing or that it carried too much risk.'

At the time he was working as a sales manager with a European technology company. Then, while he was on a business trip to South Africa in 2003, aged twenty-six, he suddenly hit crunch point and realised he absolutely had to quit his job and start a business – and embrace the risk that came with doing that. He says: 'I suddenly had this gut-wrenching realisation that I had to completely change everything right now or I would miss the boat.'

By the end of the fourteen-hour flight home Tom had decided to quit his job and had made a plan about how he was going to go about starting up his business. He decided he would spend the next three months coming up with five business ideas. Then he would choose the best one – no matter how risky or impossible it seemed – and incorporate the company and just get on with it. He had turned his approach towards risk completely on its head.

He says: 'I made the analogy that when you have a baby you don't know anything about it, yet you are committed to it from the first moment. That is the same with a company. In the past I would try to hack an idea apart until inevitably I would find a good reason not to do it. But with this one I completely committed to it even before I knew what it was, and I think that's a really important part of what drove me to do it.'

At the end of the three months, he had indeed come up with five potential business ideas, some more promising then others – one was writing a novel, one was managing his brother's band and one was something to do with insurance. Another of his ideas, the one he decided to pursue, was to start up a consumer electronics business which would sell to other retailers rather than direct to the public.

Keen to get going with his idea, Tom borrowed £23,000 from his father and began by selling a gadget he had discovered at a consumer electronics exhibition which enables people to play their iPods in the car by connecting them to the car speakers. The gadget sold well and he soon expanded into designing and developing consumer electronic products of his own, including a range of iPod docking stations. His business, Gear4, now sells products in forty countries and has a turnover of £25 million.

You can limit your risk by thinking creatively

Paul Lindley took a more cautious approach to risk when he set up his business, Ella's Kitchen, making healthy food for babies and toddlers. Paul had previously been Deputy Managing Director for Nickelodeon, the children's cable channel, before deciding to quit his job and start up his business, and he hit on a novel way of marketing his products that would not involve him spending any money. He approached all the children's television channels, proposing that they advertise his products in return for a share of his company's future revenue. Viacom, which handles the sales for Nickelodeon, agreed.

Paul says: 'It was risk-free advertising because if we sold a load of products we would give them a load of money. If we sold nothing, we would give them nothing. Initially we did a one-year deal. That gave me a piece of paper that I could go to the supermarkets with.'

He did just that and eventually Sainsbury's got in touch, saying they wanted to stock his products in four hundred stores across the country. The first range hit the shelves at the beginning of 2006.

His products were soon taken on by Tesco and Waitrose, and Paul has since launched a range of pasta sauces and healthy snacks for children. As a result, Ella's Kitchen now has sales of £20 million a year.

Remember, risk is not some immutable external force that you have automatically to accept. If you are not happy with the level of risk that starting up your business will expose you to, there are several ways of reducing that risk. You can do that, for example, by bringing in a business partner or an external investor, who will share both risk and reward. Many people feel that it is better to have a smaller slice of a large cake rather than the whole of a small cake – which could easily end up being no cake at all. How much you wish them to become involved is up to you – they may be purely an investor, or they could be an equal hands-on partner working alongside you.

You can also choose a level of ongoing risk which you are comfortable with through the strategy for growth you adopt. Deciding to supply only supermarkets, for example, may be a less risky strategy than attempting to build up a presence in independent shops and delicatessens. Your resulting profit margins could well be lower as supermarkets generally take a tough line on the price they are prepared to pay – but you may feel that that is a trade-off worth making in order to secure a long-term supply contract with a major business which is unlikely to go bust and likely to always pay on time. Calculating risk is not an exact science so the most important thing is to make sure that you are comfortable with the decisions you make.

Choose risk that fits you

Above all, make sure you start up the kind of business which mirrors your personal attitude towards risk. Not all businesses are created equal. Some businesses are inherently more risky than others because of the nature of the products they sell, and because of the way they sell them. A business that relies on constantly launching new products or new versions of the same product – a computer games company, for example, or a fashion clothing business – is going to be inherently more risky than one which sells the same product over and over again. In the same way, a business which constantly has to find new customers to buy its product – a business selling services to people moving house, for example, or one providing retirement homes for old people, is naturally going to be more risky than one which can sell to the same customers over and over again, such as a food manufacturing business.

Sorting products into needs and wants also exposes the level of risk embedded in them. When times are tough customers are always going to cut back on non-essentials such as holidays and new cars, but they are pretty much always going to need to buy tea bags and toilet rolls.

Laurence Prince, the founder of Danilo Promotions, chose an inherently risky business – making celebrity calendars. Fortunately, he positively thrives on the risk and unpredictability of his business, which by its very nature is only ever as good as the last calendar he produces. Some of his calendars have sold fantastically well – his calendar featuring the Teenage Mutant Ninja Turtles, for example, sold more than 500,000 copies, far more than anyone could have predicted. Others, though, have bombed. Laurence sold just 350 copies of his calendar featuring photos of Richard Clayderman, the pianist, even though he had printed 25,000 in anticipation of big sales. His Haircut 100 calendar would have been fantastic but for the fact that the moment the calendar hit the streets the band broke up. And he had to stop the presses rolling on his Chelsea Football Club calendar the moment he heard the news that the manager José Mourinho was no longer in the job.

Not surprisingly, over the years he has been in business Laurence has experienced a real roller-coaster ride with his venture, at one point facing debts of £1 million after the American side of his business folded, at another having to remortgage his house and put all his savings on the line. Happily, the business now has annual sales of £12 million. It would not be the kind of business that would suit most people, but Laurence has clearly loved the excitement of it all. He says: 'You need to have the knack of spotting something in the marketplace and trying to see what the trend is going to be. You must have confidence to take a risk and you have to be prepared to lose the money.'

The one thing you can never do, however, is take away the risk altogether. Business – and, indeed, life – simply does not work like that. You can take a calculated guess about which business ideas are likely to be a success and which are not, and you can narrow your selection down to something that on paper looks as though it could succeed. You can mitigate the potential risk in all the ways suggested above and you can limit your financial exposure by placing limits on what you invest and what guarantees you give.

But what you cannot do is predict with any certainty which potential business idea will definitely succeed. There are lots of business ideas which on paper looked like they would definitely succeed but flopped. And there are lots more that looked as if they would obviously fail and yet went on to succeed beyond everyone's wildest expectations. The surprise success of the O2 arena, for example, which stages concerts and events in the former Millennium Dome in London, has far surpassed anyone's expectations. So too has the success of eBay. That is the nature of the game. After all, if it was easy and painless and risk-free, then everyone would be doing it.

Finally, do not risk everything. Please don't. The stakes are simply too high and the uncontrollable unknowns simply too many. The brutal reality is that for every start-up that succeeds, two more fail, and many of those fail through no fault of their own. And if you have put everything on the line, and you lose it, you could spend the rest of your life paying for it, both literally and metaphorically.

Nick Jenkins, who founded Moonpig, the personalised greetings card company, agrees. He points out: 'If you haven't risked everything, then it isn't going to ruin your life if you fail – you can put it down to experience.' He himself invested £160,000 of money he had already earned elsewhere in his business, and then got investors to put in another £500,000, and then raised still more money from investors, keeping his own personal investment at £160,000, a level he felt comfortable and happy with. As a result his stake in the company is just 38 per cent, but it is a small stake in a lot – Moonpig now licenses eight hundred greetings card designs and has annual sales of £4.4 million.

Incidentally, several months after I advised the reader with the idea for the kitchen appliance to forget it, I got back in touch with him to find out whether he had taken my advice. Needless to say, he had not. In order to be able to support the family while he continued to pursue his dream he had now also had to sell their house in addition to their car. However, he assured me that he had so far spent only 'hundreds' pursuing his business idea and had written to several high street retailers telling them about his invention. Several months on, he had not yet heard anything back but remained optimistic that he soon would. He concluded: 'Yes, I went for it, I had to, my philosophy is regret what you don't do, not what you have done. I am a firm believer that if it is meant to be then it will happen.'

He seems like a nice man; for his sake I sincerely hope he is right and that it does all work out. I'm not holding my breath, though.

ACTION PLAN

▶▶ Investigate ways of minimising the risk within your business. Is it possible to cap the potential losses in some way?

▶▶ Decide what you are prepared to lose, then work out a worst-case scenario. If you invest £30,000 and lose it all, what happens then? Will you have to sell the family home, or will it just mean you will not be able to go on an expensive holiday for a few years? You need to be comfortable with the risk you are taking.

▶▶ Think about your personal approach to risk. Do you enjoy gambling on horses or the lottery? Have you ever bought a house with a huge mortgage when you weren't sure how you were going to pay for it? Do you gamble beyond your means or only what you can afford to lose? How does exposure to risk make you feel – do you feel energised or do you have difficulty sleeping at night?

CHAPTER 9

PUT THE RECRUITMENT CAMPAIGN ON HOLD

When Haley Hill decided to start her upmarket dating agency Elect Club from her home in south London in 2005, she realised she could not do it all by herself. Having started the business with just £1,000, however, which she used to buy a computer and print some business cards, Haley had no money to employ anyone to help her. So she decided to outsource as many functions of the business as she could to other companies which could do the work for her at an hourly or daily rate.

Haley discovered that not only could she get other companies to do her administration and book-keeping, she could also get them to do her sales, IT, accountancy, legal work, graphic design and event management. She now uses Adam Street private members' club in London as a virtual office to answer phones and collect post and as a venue for meeting new members. She uses freelance sales consultants to meet and recruit new members, and event coordinators to run events such as her Valentine's Ball. And for a while Haley even used a virtual PA in India who, because of the time difference, could work while Haley slept and so have everything ready for her the next morning.

All this has meant that, even though her dating agency has now grown to three thousand members and has a turnover of £500,000, and along the way has resulted in six marriages, thirteen engagements and two babies, Haley still only employs one person – herself.

She says: 'I started outsourcing because the business was small and had no money but now I have realised that it is actually the most efficient way to run a business. As long as clients are getting a personal service they don't really care if you have staff who are actually sitting in an office on the payroll or not.'

Haley is now even planning to franchise the business with the help of an outsourced franchise manager.

You can outsource everything these days

Once upon a time if you needed something doing in your business you really had to employ someone to do the job for you. Entrepreneurs were typically limited to being able to outsource their book-keeping and accountancy requirements. But that's just not the case any more. Advances in technology and the growing sophistication of the internet, plus the fact that a number of entrepreneurial businesses have spotted an opportunity for providing support services for other firms, have meant that these days you can outsource pretty much every function of your business, from administration to sales, from marketing and manufacturing to packaging.

Even better, by buying in services in this way you are often getting access to high-quality people who would never have agreed – or never have been able to come to work as an employee in your small fledgling business anyway. The internet, for example, makes it possible to recruit top-quality freelance programmers, web designers and translation experts from around the world.

The real benefit for a first-time entrepreneur in this arrangement is that you only pay for what you actually need. You either pay for a specific job to be done, such as designing a logo, or you pay by the day, such as for a PA, so you can increase or reduce the hours you need from week to week. That way, when times are quiet and your business has little work, you are not paying for an underused employee to sit around twiddling their thumbs all day. And that means lower overheads and far greater flexibility.

You do need to be just as rigorous in choosing an outsourcer as you would be in choosing an employee. And not only because they will be doing the work away from your office and out of your sight, so you need to feel confident that they are doing a good job, but also because in some cases they are effectively going to be representing your company – by managing your sales, or customer services,

for example. Ask around for word-of-mouth recommendations and interview several possible outsourcers before
narrowing down your choice. Always ask for references – and
follow these up – and choose on ability rather than price.
And introduce a trial period of, say, three or six months, at
the end of which you can formally review how the relationship is going.

Adam Pritchard is an entrepreneur who managed to get
a long way without staff in the first few years of starting up.
The founder of Pomegreat, the pomegranate juice sold in
major supermarket chains such as Waitrose and Tesco,
initially Adam outsourced everything including sales and
marketing, preferring to stay flexible while he was travelling
abroad to source the pomegranates he needed.

Brent and Marilena Shaw have also discovered the merits
of outsourcing. They both have separate full-time jobs and
run their online business Swiss Luggage selling luggage and
travel accessories from their home in Loughborough,
Leicestershire, working on the business in the evening and
at weekends.

When they first started their business they did all the
packing and posting of products themselves but, as sales
grew, it all started to get too much. So a year ago they decided
to outsource the packing and dispatching side of their business after realising that their time would be better spent
finding new customers. After doing some research to see
what was available they outsourced the entire fulfilment
function to a company called My Warehouse, which takes
delivery of their stock, stores it in their warehouse and
dispatches orders to customers. During the day a call centre

handles customer enquiries and deals with returns. Another bonus has been that the outsourcer is able to send out orders the same day they are received, something the Shaws were never able to do.

Brent says: 'We were very nervous initially as it was like letting go of a child and giving it to someone else to look after. But we are very happy with the arrangement and I am now a big fan of outsourcing. I think you should concentrate on the things that you are good at and let other people do the things you are not so good at. It is an effective way of working because then you get the best skills and the best knowledge, which as a small business we just couldn't do.'

An unexpected benefit of their outsourcing arrangement is that it has also solved the problem of where to store the luggage they sell – now that the outsourcer keeps it all in their warehouse, the Shaws have finally got their living room back.

Employees are a luxury you cannot afford right now

Of course, it is wonderful to be able to create new jobs and give people meaningful employment, and one day, hopefully, that is exactly what your business will do, when it is fully grown up and firmly established in its marketplace. But right now this cannot be your first priority. Employing people is a major undertaking; it involves a long-term commitment and it requires a lot of time and focus which you need to be devoting to establishing your business. What's more, taking on employees before your business is ready and able to support the cost of them could end up being a serious drain on your financial resources. Or worse.

Think about it – if you take on employees you will have to spend a lot of time, effort and money finding and recruiting them in the first place, and then more time, effort and money training them to do the job. Then, of course, you need to pay them – and on top of the basic salary you will have to pay employer National Insurance contributions, insurance and holiday pay, and set up a payroll to deduct tax and employee National Insurance contributions from their salary and forward it to the tax office. If they become sick you will have to find someone else to do their job while they are absent.

Then, if it all goes wrong, you may discover that either:

▸▸ your business is not growing as fast as you had hoped so there is not enough work for your employees to do, or

▸▸ your business has changed direction and so their skills no longer fit your requirements, or even

▸▸ they are no good at their job, in which case it is then going to take an enormous amount of time, effort and expense to part company with them.

These days there are – and rightly so – a lot of rules and regulations and red tape surrounding the employment of people. The downside to that from your point of view is that means yet more diversion of resources away from actually running your business.

On a personal level, having to let employees go whom you have come to know well can be incredibly painful too. In a small firm especially, your employees may also have become your friends and it can be really awful to have to make them redundant, particularly as you are likely to know their personal circumstances and how hard losing their job is going to affect them. Having to choose which one of two employees to let go is likely to be even more unpleasant.

Contrast all that with being able to pay for functions as and when you need them – and being able to stop paying for them instantly if you wish – and you quickly start to see why outsourcing is such an attractive proposition for fledgling businesses.

Help a graduate find a job

If you really need another pair of hands, preferably allied to an intelligent mind, then another option is to offer a graduate a temporary work placement for a few weeks. This can be a win-win situation because not only are they helping you, you are also helping them, by giving them useful, practical work experience and – hopefully – a glowing reference to put on their CV at the end of it. Depending on the type of job or skills you require – and how long you need them for – you may choose to offer the placement paid or unpaid, with expenses. There are several websites which have been set up to put small firms in touch with graduates, to the mutual benefit of both. One such website is enternships.com, where both sides specify what they are looking for and for how long. The benefit is that you can get the help you need without either side having to commit.

You must, however, make sure that you fulfil your side of the deal by providing meaningful work experience and not just a dogsbody role. And if you do decide to make the relationship more permanent, you must offer them a proper contract with a proper wage attached.

Home sweet home

A real advantage of being able to outsource many functions of your business is that you do not need to find office space for all those people you are not employing. That means that in the early days while you are getting your business off the ground you can either work from home, or from shared office space which can be rented by the month, or even from a local café. And that means lower overheads.

You will certainly be in good company. These days more than 60 per cent of all new businesses are started from home, according to Enterprise Nation, the home business website, and there are now 2.8 million home businesses in the UK, between them generating a combined annual turnover of £284 billion.

The most obvious benefit of working from home is that beyond buying a desk, installing a second phone line and stocking up on teabags, it will hardly cost you anything. It also means that you don't have to start committing to long-term rental agreements at a stage when you really have no idea how things are going to pan out. And now that technology has given small firms the opportunity to have

to stop me feeling like I am the only
, big lights, warmth, a nice view, a cup
meone to make the tea. And all for the
£1.60 it's a bargain.

ays do what Raoul Shah did. Six months
business Exposure, a creative marketing
n west London, he was so lonely working
rented a desk in the corner of a friends'
tral London. Even though the two busi-
he same industry, he was delighted to be
g office environment again.

ery conducive to my work, feeling that I
something. Even having someone to talk
while I was making a cup of tea really
t desk was a really crucial move for me
being surrounded by other people, being
don gave me a real sense of aspiration, of
ke to have an office of my own one day.
y mind on what I would love to achieve.'
the experience so enriching that Raoul,
now grown to encompass 160 employees,
workspace for other fledgling entrepre-
n office.

meanwhile, the real upside of working
ing able to outsource all the functions
ng agency has not been the convenience
r even the cost – it is that she has been
Because this way he can run around the
end or sit cheerfully at her feet wagging
y minds at all.

powerful personal computers, software and printers every bit as good and professional as those used by large corporates, there need be nothing to suggest to the outside world that your global multi-market company is actually run from your spare bedroom.

When Deborah Duddle was made redundant from her job with a workwear clothing company in 2009, she used savings of £20,000 to start her new business, Izzy and Floyd, named after her two-year-old daughter and the family dog, which sells handmade, personalised baby gifts. For Deborah, one huge benefit of running her business from home is that she can now look after Izzy instead of sending her to nursery five days a week, which she had had to do since Izzy was just a few months old. She says: 'I really missed out before. Now I can watch her growing up.'

Another real benefit of working from home is that, as Brent and Marilena Shaw of Swiss Luggage realised, you don't even have to give up your day job in order to start up a business. In fact, there are now so many people running businesses from home in their spare time in the evening and at weekends that there is even a name for them – the 5 to 9ers. The term developed from the idea that people would finish their 9 a.m. to 5 p.m. jobs and then work from 5 p.m. to 9 p.m. on their own business, although I suspect that in reality for some of them it is more like working from 5 p.m. to 9 a.m. The point is that if your office is at home you can work at three in the morning in your pyjamas if you want.

Enterprise Nation estimates that around five million people in the UK hold down day jobs while building their own company at night and at weekends. That is a lot of people. Of these, two-thirds hope the businesses they are starting will become big enough and profitable enough to enable them to switch to running them full-time within a year.

Janan Leo, twenty-nine, is a typical 5 to 9er. During the day she works as a product development manager for Virgin Trains. As soon as her day finishes there, she switches to running CocoRose, which makes foldable flat shoes for women. She started the company, which she runs from the spare room of her home in north London, in 2008 with £3,000 of savings. She works every evening from five until at least eleven o'clock, and every weekend, and now sells hundreds of pairs of shoes a month in boutiques and through her website.

She may never see her boyfriend and barely get any sleep but, for Janan, starting a business this way and running it at home has one huge advantage – it has minimised the financial risk. She says: 'I lie in bed at midnight watching the orders come through on my BlackBerry.'

Steve Emecz, thirty-eight, is another 5 to 9er running a business in his spare time from home while holding down a demanding full-time job. By day he is the Business Development Director for Venda.com, an e-commerce support company, and at night he runs MX Publishing, his own book publishing company with fifty titles ranging from Sherlock Holmes to neurolinguistics.

Steve says: 'I process urgent orders in my lunch break and normal ones in the evening. I have an outsourced warehouse that picks the books and ships them – it is all technology-driven and web-based. The authors all have day jobs themselves and so want to talk to me in the evening anyway,

and the distributors
sent direct to my Bl

But there is an

The downside of ru
it can get lonely wo
bounce ideas off or sl
When I was invited t
Business Conference
quite unlike any norma
and at first I couldn't w
excitedly to each other
leave. Then I realised t
was not just a char
speakers; it was qui
get out of the hou
Possibly for the f

If you are so
around you, ther
office space. At
you can do just
payable monthl
own, and outsid
arrangement. A
in your local c
Wi-Fi access. I
round the cor
playing in the
computer cab

laptops aroun
person in the
of tea – and e
price of the te

Or you coul
after starting u
agency, from hi
on his own tha
design agency
nesses were no
part of a stimu

He says: 'It v
was suddenly p
to for five min
helped. Renting
because, apart f
in the centre of
what it would b
It helped to focu

Indeed he fou
whose business h
now provides fr
neurs in his Lon

For Haley Hi
from home and
required by her d
or the simplicity,
able to get a dog
house for hours
his tail, and nob

ACTION PLAN

▶▶ Break down your business into functions
rather than roles. Investigate how much it
will cost to outsource each function.

▶▶ Be just as rigorous in choosing an
outsourcer as you would an employee.
Talk to several first and choose on ability
rather than price. And introduce a trial
period of, say, three or six months, after
which time you can formally review how
the relationship is going.

▶▶ Carry out an assessment of the idea of
your home as your office. Is there actually
somewhere you could put a desk? Do you
have a café or library within walking or
short driving distance where you could
escape to when you start craving
company?

▶▶ Then do the same for yourself. Will you go
mad being on your own? How disciplined
are you – are you likely to spend the day
in your pyjamas watching daytime TV
instead of chasing orders?

CHAPTER 10

SET TANGIBLE GOALS – AND AIM HIGH

Every morning as soon as he wakes up, Gavin Wheeldon, the founder of translation business Applied Language Solutions, turns on his computer and watches a five-minute PowerPoint presentation he created himself. The presentation is a reminder of all the things he wants to achieve, and a timeline showing how and when he plans to achieve them. But he has done more than simply write an abstract wish list – Gavin has also included pictures of every goal he wishes to achieve. There is a picture of the enormous house he would like to buy one day, for example, and then there is a view from the holiday home he would like to buy in Cyprus.

He says: 'I don't think that writing your goals on a piece of paper has power, whereas if you look at a picture of a mansion every day you think, I am going to get there, that is going to be mine. I really do think it works. I have never doubted where I am going.'

Gavin is clearly on to something – his business now has a turnover of £7.5 million.

Setting goals is the key to creating a successful business, and with good reason. They mark out a distinct path which could otherwise be a whirl of confusion. As the saying goes, if you don't know where you are going, you are never going to get there, and the same is true when you are starting a business. You need not only to have a strong idea of what your ultimate goal is; you need to set out smaller, regular, tangible goals along the way, both in the planning stages and once you have launched it, to ensure that you are always heading in the right direction. It's a cliché to say that every journey starts with a single step but it also happens to be true.

Where are you going today?

The benefit of setting smaller, more achievable goals as well as bigger, longer-term prizes is that they stop you becoming completely overwhelmed by what you are trying to do. It also ensures that you can see real evidence of the progress you are making, which in turn gives you the confidence to embark on the next step.

It starts from the very first moment. While you are in the planning stages, it can be all too easy to while away the days sitting in a café staring at your computer, sipping a cappuccino and fooling yourself that you are achieving something when in reality you are not. Surfing the internet, for example, is an unbelievably dangerous eater of hours. One minute you are just going online to check a single fact or to find out the price of printers, the next thing you know it is two hours later and you are somewhere deep into a holiday website dreaming of taking a trip to the Caribbean, or wondering how long it would take you to drive through Spain. I know this, because I have done it myself, many times. You can kid yourself as much as you want that it is useful and important to know the temperature in Seville in May but really it isn't, unless you are planning on starting up a travel website. And even then it is probably not top priority.

Holly Tucker and Sophie Cornish have got setting goals and making plans down to a fine art. Every January Holly and Sophie, founders of notonthehighstreet.com, which sells lifestyle goods made by small firms, shut themselves away with a pot of coffee and a pile of croissants and write a list of twelve goals for the year for their business. They begin by looking at the list they wrote the previous year and go through it point by point deciding what has been achieved, which ideas should be ditched and which should be carried over into the new year.

Holly says: 'It is a cleansing process. It is great to have it written down. We don't come out of the room until it is done. Each goal has a page and we break down that goal into what needs to be done to achieve it. Some of the ideas from 2006 have stood the test of time and are on our 2010 list. It might not have been the right time for them then but they are right for the company now.'

The idea of producing a catalogue, for example, stayed on the list for two years before they decided the time was right. The idea of exhibiting at wedding shows, which Holly and Sophie started doing in 2010, was on the list for four years.

The two women then spend a day together each month referring back to the list they made at the start of the year and discussing the long-term vision for the company. The process clearly works – in the space of just four years the business, which is based in south-west London, has gone from a turnover of zero to an expected turnover of £13.5 million in 2010.

Break it down into manageable steps

When you are in the early stages of creating a business it is a good idea to give yourself daily goals to achieve. Write a realistic 'To Do' list every evening for the next day and then break down every task into small, manageable goals. Be as precise as you can. Instead of having as your goal to get your products stocked in Waitrose, say, work out exactly which steps you will need to take in order to achieve that. You will need to contact their head food buyer, for example, and arrange for her to taste a sample of your products. You will need to have found a suitable place in which to make your products, which complies with Waitrose's health and safety regulations, and you will need to work out how many of your products you can realistically supply. You will need to source packaging and you will need to work out the shelf life of your products and where you are going to store them, and how you are going to physically deliver them to Waitrose.

If those steps are still too large, then break them down again, perhaps making it your goal to ring five packaging firms by lunchtime to ask for quotes.

Also learn to play to your strengths. If you find you work best in the morning, then start with all the hard tasks and the jobs you don't like doing, such as making phone calls. Then give yourself nice things to do in the afternoon, such as taste-testing ingredients for your cakes, when your energy is flagging. Reverse your actions if you think afternoons are when you perform best.

And don't forget to reward yourself when you manage to cross something off your list. When Robyn Jones was trying to start up her catering company Charlton House from the spare room of her home, her days consisted of cold-calling prospective clients to see if they wanted her to run their staff restaurant. It was hard going and she found it difficult to even be put through to speak to the right person, let alone get an appointment with them. This went on week after week. To force herself not to give up, she started setting herself daily goals.

She says: 'I am a very target-driven person so I would say to myself that I couldn't have a coffee until I had spoken to a prospective client and got an appointment. And then I couldn't have any lunch until I had got another one.' It worked. Her business now has an annual turnover of £76 million and clients including the American Embassy in London and the Civil Aviation Authority.

Don't set the date

When you are starting up a business the one big goal constantly at the front of your mind is the need to get everything ready in time for the launch of your business.

But stop. You need to tread carefully here. If you are launching a website-based business then having a fixed launch date set in stone is tantamount to setting yourself up to fail. That's because when technology is involved there are *always* last-minute snags and bugs that need to be ironed out. Which means there are always last-minute delays.

Holly and Sophie discovered all this the hard way when they launched notonthehighstreet.com. Holly had meticulously planned a big launch for the website. She alerted the press and potential customers well in advance and even had a microsite at the website address counting down the days. Unfortunately, and utterly inevitably, not everything went according to plan. The complex technology needed to power the website was not ready in time and so when notonthehighstreet.com launched to a great fanfare, no one could actually buy anything from it.

Holly recalls: 'We were so new to this that we didn't understand about launching with a beta version of the site. We had 16,000 people coming to the site on that first day and no one could buy anything. It was really not a good day.'

The secret to doing this well, as Holly belatedly discovered, is to have a soft launch, in which the website will quietly begin working and orders will quietly start being taken, but without any fanfare whatsoever. You can also call this the testing period or the beta launch, but the point of it is to wait until everything is working as it should be before announcing the official launch of your business.

Make sure your technology mirrors your goals

You also need to make sure your website is sufficiently equipped to help you meet your goals. Build it on a platform that will enable you to add other elements easily without having to build the entire thing from scratch. My website, rachelbridge.com, for example, is currently a very straight-forward one showing the various aspects of my work as writer, journalist and public speaker, but it has been constructed on WordPress which means that hidden below the surface is a content management system on which I could add a blog function to thrill you all with the minutiae of my daily life, if I so chose. I could also apparently get my website designers to add on an e-commerce function very easily using this system. Which means that if I wanted to I could set up an online shop and sell you T-shirts, souvenir mugs and all manner of things.

Paul Stanyer learnt the hard way about the importance of having a website that would be flexible and functional enough to meet the goals he set for his business. The idea of his business, Holiday Taxis, was that he would provide pre-booked transfers from airports to hotels overseas as an alternative for holidaymakers to joining the transfer bus which made its way slowly round all the other resorts first. He wanted customers to be able to book their transfers entirely online so he got a technology company to build him a website in return for a 20 per cent stake in the business. The website was launched in March 2003 and by May one thousand travel agents had registered. But in June Paul hit a big problem. When he designed the website he had presumed that the majority of his customers would want to book standard-sized taxis to take them to their hotels and so the website would only allow them to do that. But instead large numbers of people were booking vehicles with more seats, something they could only do over the phone.

He says: 'We were in danger of becoming a call centre, which defeated the objective of being a technology-based solution.' Worse than that, the website had been constructed in such a way that it was impossible elegantly to add on a function to allow large vehicles to be selected.

After a lot of agonising, Paul decided that, rather than bolt on new technology to his existing website, it would be far more sensible to rebuild it entirely. As a result he was not able to promote the company until his website was fully functional and had to endure an agonising wait for a couple of months until the website was ready and he could get on with promoting his business again. Fortunately he has since made up for lost time. Holiday Taxis now has sales of £21 million and operates in more than seventy countries.

Have a vision

Once you have launched your business you still need to set regular milestones to achieve, although by now they are likely to be weekly and monthly rather than daily. But alongside that, you also need to have a long-term vision for the business too. It can be tempting to think that having a vision and a strategy is purely something that large corporates do. But it is actually vitally important for all businesses, no matter how new or small they are.

If you don't know how or where to start, just get a blank sheet of paper and write down where you want your business to be in five years' time and how you want it to look. Do you want to be selling overseas, for example? Do you want to have expanded into new areas, or to have added to your product range? Remember, there are lots of paths you could potentially take so it is important to think about all the options and decide which would make more sense for you and your business. If you are starting out selling children's clothes, for example, is the long term plan to expand into other products for children, such as toys, or is it to expand into ranges of clothing for adults? Or would you like to expand the business into running workshops to show other people how to make children's clothes of their own? There are no right or wrong answers, and you can always change direction later, but it is good to spell out from the outset what direction you want to take otherwise you will quickly get lost and distracted. Putting the emphasis on the clothes side of the concept, for example, is very different from putting the emphasis on the children's side of the equation and will dictate everything from how your website will look to which retail shops you target to stock your range.

If the goals you have set yourself overwhelm you, then once again break them down until they become more manageable. The idea of selling 100,000 widgets a year may sound utterly impossible, for example, but if you break it down that is only equivalent to selling 274 widgets a day – which suddenly sounds a lot more manageable. All successful businesses incorporate long-term planning as a continual part of their thinking. It is the difference between being on a raft on a river that takes you where it wants to go, and being on a boat with an outboard motor and it going where you want to go.

Consider your personal goals too

Barbara Froomberg cheerfully confesses that the reason she started her business Safety First Aid, which provides safety products and first aid training equipment to firms, was because she wanted to send her three children to private school. She was spurred into action when her husband changed jobs and took a large pay cut and she realised she needed to do something big in order for them to be able to afford to do it. Barbara actually started by buying a tiny first aid business that sold plasters and bandages to the building trade for £800, which her mother lent her. That provided her with a business name, one customer, a few small orders that had to be sent out and sales of £3,500 a year. With no knowledge of running a business, Barbara sat at home for three weeks and wondered what to do. Then she put on a safety helmet, put a stretcher on her shoulder and started knocking on the doors of companies that might want to buy from her. She has since managed to build it up into a £9 million business, and along the way did indeed manage to put all three children through private education.

Don Lewin, meanwhile, started up Clinton Cards partly to fulfil a childhood dream of owning a Rolls-Royce. He finally achieved his ambition at the age of forty, having started and built up the business from scratch. He had to go up to Manchester to collect his brand new Rolls-Royce and pay an extra £2,000 to take immediate delivery because there was a waiting list. But it was worth it, he says: 'It was a great day. Ever since I was a child my ultimate ambition had been to own a Rolls-Royce. I felt I had arrived.'

There was just one problem in having achieved his dream, he says – he now needed a new challenge. So he set himself the target of making a huge amount of money. As he explains: 'You always need a goal in life.' He has managed to achieve that, too – Clinton Cards now has 860 shops in the UK and the Republic of Ireland and annual sales of around £400 million.

Reach for the stars

Finally, and perhaps most important of all, think big and aim high – and then set your goals accordingly. Don't limit yourself to doing something small when you could be doing something big and changing the world. After all, what is the real difference between selling to a thousand customers and selling to a million, other than a few zeros? (Yes, all right, I know there's a bit more to it than that . . .)

What is that old saying? Whether you think you can, or whether you think you can't, you are right? It's not just words; you really can be the next Richard Branson or Anita Roddick if you want to be. You just have to think big and go for it. If you have a great idea then don't hide it and limit its potential; get it out there into the world so we can all enjoy it. Now start making that list.

ACTION PLAN

▶▶ Stick a picture on your fridge of something big you would like to achieve.

▶▶ Write a list of your long-term goals for the business. Be as specific as you can. Then break them down into more practical milestones. Then date it so you can revisit it and update it every year.

▶▶ Think about your personal goals as well as your aims for the business. Your goal might purely be to make lots of money, but also think about why you want that money and what you are going to spend it on and what difference it is going to make to your life. The more tangible and real you can make your goal, the easier it will be to imagine it and to achieve it.

CHAPTER 11

LET GO OF PERFECT – IMPERFECT CAN BE EVEN BETTER

When Vanita Parti decided to start up her business Blink brow bars, stand-alone eyebrow-threading bars which would be located in big department stores, she had it all mapped out in her mind.

She wanted to keep her business small and perfect and when she had managed to open three eyebrow bars in three top London locations – Selfridges, Fenwick and Harvey Nichols – she was delighted. She had the business she had always dreamed of and had no great desire to expand it further.

She was getting calls every week from department stores around the country begging her to set up a Blink eyebrow-threading bar for them, too, but she turned them all down.

She says: 'I had stores calling from Colchester to Newcastle but I said no because I was so worried about jeopardising quality. Selfridges used to ring me up and say, come on, get up to Manchester and I would say, if I can't give you the best service I am not going to do it.'

But then other people saw how well Vanita's three eyebrow bars were doing and they saw the queues of customers waiting to have their eyebrows threaded. And very soon copycat eyebrow-threading bars were popping up all over the place. Even worse from Vanita's point of view was that, once a department store had one eyebrow-threading bar in place, they had no need or desire for a second.

It was at this point that Vanita suddenly realised she had got it all wrong. That instead of keeping her business the size it was, she should have been busy opening new Blink bars across the country as fast as she could before anyone else could get a toehold in the market.

She says: 'In hindsight I think I was too emotional about it. I was a little precious about it because I was so concerned about the brand being perfect. I should have been more of a businesswoman and said, look, let's just get in there and then I will deal with the quality issues.'

Luckily for her, there was still some room left in the market for new Blink bars. She now has ten across the country, all of which she has developed to the same high standard as the first bar, and an annual turnover of £3 million.

Vanita was extremely fortunate that she was able to

embrace realism and catch up in time before she was completely sidelined from the market that she herself had created. But many others are not.

When you are starting up a business for the first time, it is natural to want to try to make everything perfect, for the very fact that it is your first time and because you want everything about your business to be the best it can be. And also because you are terrified that if you don't get it absolutely right from the word go then failure will automatically ensue.

Unfortunately, new businesses can be a lot like toddlers – unruly, difficult to control and liable to run off in the opposite direction without warning. Much as you might like the idea of being in control, your business will quickly develop a life of its own and often initially all you can do is hang on for the ride and endeavour to keep up. Trying to make everything perfect will only lead you down a path of frustration and misery and banging your head against a brick wall.

It's OK not to be perfect

The good news is that you don't actually need to make everything perfect right from the start. In fact, there are many benefits to *not* getting it right first time.

The first step is to realise that everything is a work in progress, and that that is a good thing. Doing things imperfectly keeps the door open to new ideas and new possibilities and gives you the freedom to improve on your original idea. There is no greater motivator than the idea of striving for perfection, even if you never actually achieve it. The moment you think you have everything perfect is the moment you and your business slide into complacency. And complacency is fatal.

Of course, I am not talking about doing things in a slip-shod manner. That is the fastest possible way to send your business crashing to the floor. And if you are making a product or providing a service, then it needs to be the best it can be. If you are making and selling food, for example, you are not going to get very far if you start giving your customers food poisoning. But it is important to think about what is truly important to your business and what is merely a sideshow. In Vanita's case the most important thing, the central core on which her business rested, was that her staff could do eyebrow threading brilliantly and fabulously. What was not so important was that they had uniforms that matched those of staff in other department stores, for example, or that the chairs were the same colour. Or that she opened her Blink bars in a coherent, orderly way across the country.

Steve Jobs, Bill Gates and Homer Simpson can't all be wrong

The problem with being a perfectionist is that you would never actually launch anything onto the market for fear of it being less than perfect. The world of technology and computing is a good example. Steve Jobs at Apple would never have launched any products if he was waiting and striving to produce the best one ever, quite simply because he is never going to be able to get to that point. More importantly, it was only by bringing out the first Apple computer, or the first iPod, that he could see how customers reacted to it and find out which aspects of it worked and which didn't, and which functions needed to be improved, or removed, or expanded. Indeed, with the iPhone, the things that were missing from it have gone on to spawn a whole new business opportunity – Apps, software which you can download onto your iPhone to help you do everything from finding a recipe for chocolate fudge cake to getting the latest weather report for your region.

Every time Microsoft launches new computer software there are always things that are imperfect about it, and bugs that need ironing out. Indeed, the Microsoft adverts for Windows 7, collectively called My Idea, were based entirely on the concept of different people asking for their new computer to be better than their old one, by starting up faster and having new task bars and so on. But if Bill Gates had waited until he had perfect software before launching it onto the market, we would all still be waiting and the world would be a very different place.

Closer to home and on a smaller scale, a cake shop can only find out how good its cakes are and how it can make them better by actually selling them and then listening to customers' opinions about them. The feedback is what makes a business great.

Sometimes you consciously have to stop trying to mould your product to fit how you want it to be and instead just go with the flow and follow where it wants to take you. When the cult TV show *The Simpsons* first began, its creator,

Matt Groening, initially cast Bart, the wayward son, as the main character. Most of the shows in the first few seasons had storylines centred around Bart and he was the focus of most of the merchandise, as well as two music videos. But as audiences for the show grew it became clear that the well-meaning but flawed father Homer was more popular than Bart, that people identified with him and were more interested in what happened to him. So, rather than doggedly sticking to his original premise of the show being all about Bart, the creator simply switched the focus to Homer. As a result *The Simpsons* has become one of the most successful television shows of all time, and is still running after more than twenty years.

The problem with trying to be a perfectionist in business is that it implies that there is some way of controlling all the unknown elements that go towards creating perfection, when in reality there is not. If you are going to start up a business you need to accept right from the start that it is simply not going to turn out how you imagine it will.

When mobile phones were first launched, for example, no one had any idea that texting would become such an important part of how people would use their phones. Indeed, initially texting was not even considered a commercial application; it was merely designed as a way for phone-testing engineers to be able to contact each other. But consumers loved it so much that mobile phone designers had to start thinking about ways to make texting easier and more user-friendly on their phones, and mobile phone operators had to react to the demand by changing the way they priced the usage of their phones to include it. Today three-quarters of all mobile phone users in the world also send texts.

Sometimes you just have to go with the flow

When Stuart Miller started up his business ByBox he thought he knew exactly how it was going to turn out. At the age of thirty-two he realised the internet was starting to take off and he decided online shopping was an opportunity he could not afford to miss. So his big idea was to provide a bank of boxes nationwide where delivery companies could leave customers' products that had been ordered from online retailers.

He says: 'It was clear that if the whole online shopping thing happened in the way people were predicting, there was no way the distribution end of that could sustain it. Everyone would be driving around trying to deliver to people who weren't at home. I thought you could have a bank of boxes like left-luggage lockers, so companies such as DHL could deliver into these boxes, even in the middle of the night, and then send the customer a text message.'

Several years and a lot of changes of direction later, Stuart's business is a big success with an annual turnover of £35 million. But along the way it has morphed into an entirely different business; instead of dealing with retail customers, he deals with corporate customers, and instead of owning a bank of boxes, he has moved into distribution, delivering spare parts for mobile engineers to boxes in petrol stations.

At a more basic level, you have to accept that not every-thing is going to go right all the time, no matter how much you want it to. When Andy Drake started up his business RTG, selling promotional merchandise, he had to learn quickly that sometimes things don't go quite the way you would like. One day he was waiting for a shipment of 100,000 promotional T-shirts to arrive from Bangladesh when the transport company phoned and told him to switch on the television. Andy turned on the news just in time to see the ship carrying his consignment ablaze off Felixstowe.

Another time, he was asked to supply 500,000 T-shirts as part of a beer promotion. The idea was that the garments would be made in Bangladesh and then printed in Plymouth. But when the clothes arrived, they were soaking wet because their container had been damaged in transit. They were taken away by insurers and never seen again.

Other setbacks have included suppliers putting the wrong logos on a consignment of shirts, a container of goods falling off a ship and designs looking as though a child had done them with a potato at nursery school.

But Andy persevered and took the setbacks in his stride and RTG now has a turnover of around £10 million a year.

Don't be a perfectionist, be a realist, with a healthy dollop of self-deprecating humour thrown in. It will save your sanity and, hopefully, also your business.

If you are not expecting things to be perfect, it also makes it easier to deal with and learn from mistakes. And the one thing an entrepreneur absolutely needs to be able to do is to accept, firstly, that mistakes are going to be made – both by themselves and by others. Then, secondly, to rectify them, to learn from them and to move on. If you get stuck in a circle of self-loathing and personal blame every time you get something wrong – or, even worse, if you start blaming everyone else – then either you need to stop doing that right now, or you need to think hard about whether you are really cut out for this. To be a successful entrepreneur you need to be able to allow yourself to make mistakes, and then you need to be able to learn from them and to move on from them.

Failure is life's way of saying you must do better next time

At its most extreme this may mean accepting that your first attempt at starting a business has been a huge and utter failure. Indeed, behind every successful entrepreneur there is almost always at least one failed business somewhere along the line. When Jeremy Harbour's first business, an amusement arcade and takeaway-food operation, failed after eighteen months when he was nineteen, swallowing his entire life savings, he unsurprisingly did not take it well. 'I stopped eating for weeks,' he says. 'I went very pale and gaunt and my weight fell to about eight stone. I had to move back in with my parents and I pretty much stayed in my room for three months and didn't talk to anyone.'

His next venture was also a failure. He started up a telecoms company which he grew ambitiously for eight years. But the business was always undercapitalised and had to be rescued by an outside investor, with the result that Jeremy lost a million pounds. Happily, he is now busy proving that third time really can be lucky. He runs a company which buys and sells businesses and has so far carried out more than 20 transactions.

He says: 'Failure taught me that the downside isn't actually as bad as the thought of the downside, so the juice is probably worth the squeeze. Failure is all part of the journey of life. Emotionally it might tear you apart, but when you rationalise it, failure doesn't really mean anything. It's not tangible. It's not like you've lost a leg'

There is a wonderful phrase they use in America to describe business failures – they call it the million-dollar MBA. In other words, the fact that your business failed is not a cause for shame and embarrassment, it is an acknowledgement that you have learnt an enormous amount from the experience of setting up and running a business, which is equal to having done an MBA. Yes, the cost of doing a normal MBA would probably have been significantly less than the million dollars or whatever amount you lost when your business failed, but that's the point at which you have to be able to take a step back and laugh at yourself and the absurdity of it all.

Finally, whatever you do, don't wait for the perfect moment in your life to start your business. If you try to do that then quite simply your business is destined to remain a figment of your imagination. If you wait for that elusive calm moment when you have moved house, or finished having babies, or the children have left school, or you have saved up enough money, or when no relatives need looking after, then you are never actually going to start up your business. You might as well wait for the time when everyone is happy and the sun is shining and there is world peace and life is discovered on Mars . . . you get the general idea. The fact is this perfect moment is never going to arrive so you might as well give up waiting for it.

Just do it. Now

So forget about trying to quantify and evaluate all the external factors crowding into your decision-making. The very best time to start a business is when you suddenly and very strongly get that now-or-never feeling and you can't shake it off. That if you don't do it now, then you never will.

When Mike Clare started up his business selling beds, his wife was pregnant with their first child, they were in the process of moving house and he had to give up a good job as an area manager for a large chain of furniture stores. He said: 'It was not the best time to start my own business and put everything on the line, but my wife was very supportive and said that if it failed and we were going to have hard times then it was better to do it now rather than later.' Happily for Mike and his wife, his business, Dreams, was a huge success and he sold it several years later for more than £200 million.

And when Penny Streeter started up her business Ambition24hours, providing temporary staff for nursing homes, the timing was even less ideal. Penny, who was born in the UK but brought up in South Africa, found herself at a difficult point in her life. Her first business, a recruitment agency, had failed, her marriage had broken down, she was pregnant with her third child and had so little money that she and her children were living in accommodation for the homeless provided by the council. But, despite all this, she knew she wanted to try starting up a business again. She admits: 'My mother said, don't be ridiculous. But I knew we could do it. I felt that I had nothing to lose.'

She started the business up with her mother, the two of them working alternate days so that they could share childcare. For the first few years money was so tight that to make ends meet they had to work every weekend playing music at children's parties. Penny says: 'We had no money and we didn't want to go to the bank because we thought they would laugh us out of the door.' But in spite of the hurdles her business has thrived and now has annual sales of £65 million.

The fact is that if you are going to do it – and I mean actually do it instead of just endlessly talking about it – then you have to throw yourself in and do the best you can regardless of whatever is going on around you. We all know people who go on and on about things they are going to do one day. And we all know that they are probably never actually going to get round to doing them. The hardest thing about starting a business is actually starting it. So do that bit and forget about trying to make it perfect from day one.

It's like the old National Lottery slogan, which I have always loved for its simplicity (rather than the fact that I have never won more than £10 in the lottery): you have to be in it to win it. Procrastination stops 99 per cent of would-be entrepreneurs from ever taking the plunge. Don't let yourself be one of them.

ACTION PLAN

▶▶ Choose a name for your business that is flexible and non-specific enough to withstand unplanned changes in direction of your products or services.

▶▶ Set up a system to enable you to get instant feedback from your customers about your business which you can then use to tweak your product or service. This could be as simple as sending an email a few days after your products have been delivered asking for customers' views. Make sure your request is not intrusive or annoying, and give them an incentive to complete it, such as 10 per cent off their next order.

▶▶ Write down what you feel are the key elements of what you are trying to do and the core values you wish your business to have. That way you can allow your business to change and morph and still know that its essence remains intact.

CHAPTER 12

CHERISH YOUR (NET) PROFIT

The first two words you need to learn when starting a business are *net profit*. There is no point in putting all this effort into starting a business if you are trying to sell a product or service that you are hardly going to make any money on. It will take you until you are old and grey to make any kind of progress at all.

Doing business is not about how many widgets you can sell; it is about how much net profit you can make on the sale of each widget. If you are not actually making any profit, then you do not have a business – you have a hobby. Or, as the old saying goes, turnover is vanity, profits are sanity.

But first, a quick accounting lesson: gross profit is the difference between the amount it costs you to make or buy your products and the amount you are able to sell them on to customers for. Net profit is gross profit minus overheads, in other words the profit after all the costs of running the business have been subtracted. Gross profit shows you how much mark-up you are able to put on your products, but net profit is what you are really interested in. You can have a fantastic gross profit but if your running costs are sky high then you could end up with no net profit at all.

When Aamir Ahmad started up his first business, a mail-order furniture company, he devoted seven years of his life and a huge amount of money – both his and other people's – to making it work. But it ended in disaster because the profits just weren't there to be had. No matter how big he grew the business and no matter how much energy he put into it, there was not enough of a difference between the price he paid to buy the furniture from the manufacturers and the price he could sell it on to customers. In other words, the structure of the business meant that it could never make any money. Aamir struggled on but eventually he was forced to give up when investors refused to put in any more money and the business was sold for a knock-down price.

He says: 'Looking back, it is quite astonishing how badly planned it was. The business grew faster and faster but we weren't really making any money, we were banking on the fact that the business would grow even more. But I had built a business which was never really focused around making money, it was all about growing sales. It got to the stage where we were doubling in size year on year and we had a hundred employees but I still hadn't built a business that was making money. The business was structured really badly and I just got it completely wrong.'

Happily for Aamir, he didn't give up there. After taking time out to recover from the experience, he started another furniture business, Dwell, which now has nineteen stores and an annual turnover of £35 million. And, more importantly, the new business started making profits within seven months of opening and has never stopped making profits since.

He says: 'The most important thing was I started the business with more of a focus on making money.'

Make sure you are adding value

So how do you ensure that there is going to be enough of a profit in your business for you to hold on to? The first thing to do is to decide how you are going to add value to what you are selling. If you are making the products yourself then this bit is obvious. A beautifully decorated cake has obviously had value added to it since it started out as eggs and flour. Ditto a handmade greetings card since it started out as a piece of card and some coloured pens. But what if you are simply selling other people's products? That is what Amazon is doing, after all, and so is lastminute.com. Then you need to add value in the way you sell them. Provide your customers with the ease of a one-stop online shop, for example, so they can find everything they need in a particular category in one place. Or provide them with additional services, such as customer reviews or special discounts, or faster delivery times, which they could not get if they shopped for the products elsewhere. You can be as creative as you like here. But if you are selling a product that people could just as easily buy elsewhere then you have got to give them a reason to choose to buy from you. If the added-value bit is something special that only your business knows how to do then so much the better. Profit margins are the essence of a successful business and you need to protect yours as much as you possibly can.

If you are selling other people's products or services you also need to work out exactly where you will slot into the selling chain which runs from manufacturer to customer – and whether there is going to be enough profit margin left for you to make it worth your while. If the industry is set up so that the manufacturer sells to a national wholesaler who sells to a local distributor who sells to the customer, for example, that is already a lot of people in the chain taking their slice of profits and it is going to be hard to take another slice out for you.

If, say, the manufacturer buys his raw materials for £1 and sells his finished product to a wholesaler for £2, and the wholesaler sells it to a distributor for £4 and the distributor sells it to the retailer for £6, and the retailer sells it to customers for £10, you can see that, while everyone in the chain gets a slice of gross profit on each product, there isn't much scope for anyone else in the chain to make a sizeable gross profit themselves. If you are planning to replace the retailer and sell to the customer then it is easy to see where your profit will come from. And, even better, if you are planning to buy direct from the manufacturer and cut out the wholesaler and distributor, it is plain to see where you could potentially get lots of profit. But if you are planning to be merely another link in the chain, selling to other businesses who will then sell on, then you need to make sure there will be enough of a slice of profit to make it worth your while.

Now work out your profit margins

The next thing you need to do is look closely at your costs. If you are planning to start up a business selling hats, for example, work out how much you will be able to sell your hats for and how much they will cost to make. Then add in everything from marketing costs and delivery costs to the cost of heating and lighting. And don't forget to include *all* the costs, from the petrol that goes into the delivery van to the cost of phone calls to the cost of the hat boxes. No cost is too small to include – you may not think it is worth including your plastic bags at 10p a go, but you will when you are getting through five thousand of them a year at a total cost of £500.

If your costs work out to be more than the price you are planning to sell your product or service at, then either go back and re-examine your costs and work out how to reduce or eliminate them – or forget the whole idea. It is as simple as that, but you would be surprised how many people start businesses without even thinking about this. No profits equals no viable business. End of story.

One word of caution here: when people start working out how much a product has cost them to make, or how much a service has cost them to provide, they often forget about how much their own personal involvement is costing them. If, for example, you want to start up a business cleaning windows for £10 an hour, you might point to the mop and bucket of soapy water and conclude that for every hour you work you are making a profit of, say, £8, after taking into account the cost of the mop and the bucket and the cost of driving your van to the job, which costs you £2. But you have forgotten to include the cost of your labour. And while you might be happy not to pay yourself – because you are growing a business that will ultimately have value – you would definitely have to pay someone else to do the job instead of you. If, for example, it would cost you £7 an hour to pay someone else to clean the windows for you – while you are off drumming up more business, for example – then your profit would instantly drop to just £1 a hour. And if the cost of hiring window cleaners goes up to £8 an hour, you can see that all your profit would instantly be wiped out. You must include the cost of labour otherwise the minute you need to take yourself out of it the whole basis of the business will collapse.

How to charge a premium

There is, of course, also the question of why anyone would pay your business £10 an hour to have their windows cleaned rather than paying a casual window cleaner £8 an hour. Customers may be happy to do so, perhaps because you are more reliable, or you have a better booking system, or because your company does the job better, but you need to be clear about why you are going to be able to charge a premium.

Pimlico Plumbers are a brilliant example of how this can work in practice. The last time my boiler broke down I called Pimlico Plumbers to fix it, even though I knew they would charge an absolute fortune. It cost me £202 for them to do 20 minutes' work, which was really painful. The reason I called them was not because I had £202 sitting around that I didn't much care about, but because, having used them several times before, I knew that they would turn up when they said they would, that they would do the job properly – and that if they didn't then I knew where to find them to get them to come back and do it again. Pimlico Plumbers charge at least 50 per cent more than the local competition, in my experience, and so can you for your service, but only if you offer the quality of service and the reliability to justify a customer paying it.

You get what you pay for

The saying goes 'you get what you pay for' and in general it is true. The more desirable your product, the more you can charge. Think about all the things you buy in your life that you spend more on than you strictly need to. Do you buy your groceries at Waitrose rather than Aldi, for example? Do you take the train or plane to see your relatives in Edinburgh rather than going by coach? Do you get your carpets cleaned by professionals rather than doing it yourself? There are lots of things in life that we buy not because of price, but because we like them for other reasons, some practical, some emotional, some downright silly. But we still do it, and these are the types of products and services that first-time entrepreneurs should be looking at because the potential for adding value is greater.

You may also want to think about where the real profits are made in the industry you are planning to enter. Take chocolate, for example. You can make a profit margin by buying it from a wholesaler and then selling it on in a shop or via your website, but you can make a much bigger profit by making the chocolate yourself and then selling it. That way you get to pick up two lots of profit margins and have the added bonus of controlling the whole process from start to finish. Which means you can be absolutely sure that your chocolate is going to be made the way you want it to be made. This is what Helen and Simon Pattinson discovered when they started up their chocolate business, Montezuma's, in 2000. They initially planned simply to open a shop and sell high-quality chocolate made by British suppliers. But just before their shop was due to open, their leading supplier, who was going to be providing 50 per cent of their products, went bust. So the Pattinsons decided to make the chocolate themselves, a move which in retrospect has been the making of the business as it means their profit margins are substantially higher. Not only that, but it has opened up a whole new sales route for them and now most of their sales are made from selling the chocolate they make to wholesalers.

Because you're worth it

Whatever you do, make sure you don't undercharge for your product or service. You will be doing yourself absolutely no favours if you do. First-time small business owners have a tendency to undercharge for their services because they are very conscious that they are small and new and they don't want to look cheeky or bold or audacious. But as a general rule customers see price as a reflection of quality and, if you charge too little, they will see your products as being of inferior quality. Or, worse, they will see a business that does not value itself and believe in its products – and therefore one that is likely to fail.

Do not be apologetic about your first business. You either believe in it and think it has real worth and merit and will add something good to people's lives, or you don't. If you do, then be robust in sticking up for it and fighting its corner, and if you don't, go and do something else instead. Otherwise you will be wasting your time.

The other big mistake first-timers make is to think that they can start off by charging a low price to gain a foothold in the market and then gradually increase their prices as they become more established. But it doesn't work that way. If you enter the market at a certain price level then that is the level that customers will associate with your product and will expect to pay. Raising prices is notoriously difficult unless customers can see that there is a really good reason why prices have gone up – that the product has become significantly better, for example. And even that can be really difficult. Once customers become used to the idea of paying a certain price for something, they can be very resistant to the idea of change.

If you really think that going in with a low price will be a good idea then start by offering customers an introductory deal for a limited period only, and make it absolutely clear and be strict about when that period will end. But it is a risky business to overtly link your product or service intrin-sically to price at all – if people are only buying your product because it is cheap, they will instantly disappear when they decide it is no longer cheap, whereas what you should be aiming for is to build a strong brand loyalty among customers so that they will make your product or service part of their lives and buy it regardless of price.

A well-known pizza chain made this mistake. When they first started offering a two-for-one deal on pizzas for people dining in their restaurants who had collected a voucher from a national newspaper, everyone got very excited and rushed down to take advantage of the deal, because the pizzas were good and because two for one is a pretty good offer. But as time went on, the offer became ubiquitous, and soon anyone who was eating in the pizza houses was bearing a two-for-one voucher. Customers became so used to getting the deal that it stopped being special and people no longer regarded it as a treat. It became the norm instead. By making the offer a quasi-permanent one, the pizza chain had effectively halved the price that people were willing to pay for their pizzas and presumably eaten sharply into their profit margins.

Or take a well-known chain of sofa shops which seems to have a permanent half-price sale on, to the extent that it seems unlikely that anyone could actually buy a sofa there at full price, even if they wanted to. Presumably the company does not ever seriously expect anyone to buy one of their sofas at full price and has factored this into their business model, but it still seems to be a funny way to do business.

It pays to be exclusive

Exclusive equals profit margins and, for the brave and bold, there are all sorts of ways to get this right. When Emma Bridgewater started selling her range of painted cups and plates to department stores, she took the deliberate decision to set the price extremely high, at twice that of her competitors. People told her she was mad and that no one would buy her stuff, but in fact the opposite has happened – by pricing her products so high, Emma gave them an exclusive cachet which turned them into highly desirable collectors' items to be bought for special occasions. And in the process she also managed to attract lots of media attention from journalists wondering what the fuss was all about. Pricing her products so high also had another advantage – in the early days it kept the volume of orders at a level that Emma was able to cope with without becoming overwhelmed. Now, several years on, her products are still priced far higher than the competition's, and they are also the most well-known too, with customers deliberately seeking out her distinctive spotted plates and bowls. Her business, Emma Bridgewater, has a turnover of £8 million and goes from strength to strength.

Remember – and this is important – you don't have to churn out thousands of your products every week to make a business work. In fact, if you can charge a higher price for your products than the market would suggest, either because your products are more exclusive, or better made, or because your service is far superior to the competition's, then as a first-time entrepreneur that can be a very appealing prospect. It certainly will be appealing if it means you can keep the volumes low enough to run the business from home for the first year before having to take the plunge and rent a warehouse and a factory, or having to take out a huge bank loan to cover cash flow. That way you can take your time to get it right without the pressure on you to instantly churn out a mountain of orders.

The bottom line is that this is not a numbers game, it is a profits game. And when the time comes for you to sell your business for vast amounts of money, it will be margins that your purchasers will be interested in, not the fact that you need a warehouse the size of a football pitch to store all your measly-margined products in.

ACTION PLAN

▶▶ Make sure you really understand the concepts of profit and loss, margins, turn-over and retail sales. Go online, buy a book, attend an evening class, but do not proceed until you can tell your gross profit from your net profit.

▶▶ Write down how much your product or service is going to cost. Include everything, no matter how trivial it might seem.

▶▶ Go out into the high street or local shopping centre and look at the prices being charged for products similar to your own. Think about whether you would be able to charge more, or less, and, either way, why.

▶▶ If you are buying a ready-made product from someone else to sell on, ask yourself what value you are really adding to it. Think about whether the manufacturer could simply decide to sell direct to the customer one day and cut you out of the chain altogether.

CHAPTER 13

ASK FOR HELP

When James Hibbert started his bespoke tailoring service Itsuits, he found it really hard going. To get the business off the ground he and his business partner Shirley Biggs put in £5,000 each and went to see a manufacturer who taught them how to measure somebody for a suit. Then they each called up fifteen friends and offered to make them a bespoke suit in the hope that, if they liked them, they would recommend the service to other people.

It was a disaster. 'Ten of the suits didn't fit at all,' says James. 'Our friends were saying, what on earth are you doing? We had to do a lot of remakes.'

They got the suits right eventually, but the first year was a real slog, resulting in sales of £87,500. The second year was even harder and sales actually fell, to £72,000.

'It was pretty demotivating,' says James. Having saved only three months' salary from his previous job to live on while the business got going, he was soon struggling and was forced to remortgage his house twice. By the end of the second year the business was close to insolvency and James realised he had to take action, fast.

He decided to change the name of the company to Dress2Kill and start again with a fresh approach. Desperate for advice on how to turn the company round, he wrote to Virgin boss Sir Richard Branson and to Charles Dunstone, the founder of Carphone Warehouse, asking them if he could have an hour of their time in return for making them a suit. He did not know either of them personally yet both agreed and within a week James had met both men.

'I didn't know them at all, but I went to see them and they were brilliant,' he says.

Richard Branson offered to let James promote his bespoke service in the Virgin Upper Class airport lounge and put him in touch with Virgin Brides, where James offered his services to grooms. And Charles Dunstone gave him sound advice when they met, too. Inspired by the advice he received, James took a short course at Cranfield School of Management and completely revamped the business, improving Dress2Kill's website and kitting out a shop where customers could be fitted for a suit in pleasant surroundings while having a glass of champagne. It proved to be a turning point for the business which now has a turnover of £5 million a year.

When you are running a small business it is tempting to think you can and should do everything yourself. There is an enduring image of the lone entrepreneur striding forth and tackling every challenge in his or her path, and it can feel like a weakness to admit that you cannot solve every problem yourself. But let me tell you now, that image is a myth. Whenever I ask successful entrepreneurs the secret of their success, they almost always say it is partly down to the team of people they have assembled around them. They are not simply being generous, they are being truthful. Behind every successful entrepreneur there is a team working hard to help them. Journalists tend not to write about the team, because they are not the interesting part of the story, but they are real and they exist.

You too need to create a support team of people around you, one which is made up both of people who can give you practical help in the early days of starting out, such as helping you to stick labels on envelopes and pack boxes, and people who can offer you informed advice based on knowledge and experience.

It can be hard to admit you need help, particularly if you are surrounded by people who already think you are completely idiotic to be trying to do what you are doing. But practical help can make an amazing difference in getting things done. And advice from someone who has been there before can make a huge difference to your chances of success, not least because you will, hopefully, avoid the pitfalls they encountered.

All you have to do is ask

Now I'm not suggesting that you all start writing to Richard Branson or Charles Dunstone to ask for an hour of their time. They will probably not thank me if you do. But the good news is that there are plenty of other people closer to home who will be happy to offer advice. What about your former boss, or a former colleague, or a lecturer from your business evening class? Or the head of the local trade association? You'd be amazed how pleased people are to share their knowledge. Those who aren't will quickly make it obvious – by not answering your emails or phone calls – and you can move on.

If you don't know of anyone yourself, start going to networking events in your area organised by your local Business Link, Enterprise Agency, or Chambers of Commerce. You can gain an enormous amount of help and advice by joining a networking organisation, both through the workshops and seminars they put on and also by the people you meet there. Trade and industry fairs are also a good way to meet experts in your field. If you find someone whose advice you would value, then ask them if they would mind sparing half an hour of their time for a chat over coffee. They can always say no.

These days, as well as real-life, face-to-face networking organisations, you also have the option of virtual online networking organisations, something which can be particularly useful if you are geographically remote. If you run your business from home, for example, then Enterprise Nation, the home business network, is a mine of useful information and practical advice, and has a forum page where you can ask other members for help and advice on particular issues.

Some entrepreneurs such as Heather Bestel have found online social networking to be an amazing source of help and advice. Heather runs her psychotherapy and stress-management firm, A Little Bit of Me Time, from her home, a remote farmhouse in south-west Scotland, selling relaxation CDs and providing advice over the phone, so she relies a lot on getting help via the internet instead of meeting people face to face. She says: 'I have joined lots of internet

far better to get advice from five different people
one person dry of information and make them
d never met you. Be polite, be succinct, be
on't outstay your welcome, either literally or
, and you will find people are often willing
nd point you in the right direction.

an investment

ur business needs more than simply free,
you may find it worth paying for some
ce. This is what Sumir Karayi did. When
computer company 1E – named after a
in 1998, he initially ran the business as
une in partnership with two former

up in the Indian city of Mussoorie and
with his family at the age of fourteen,
that we'd be a commune of the top
our field and that everyone in the
equal.'
put in £500 each and ran the venture,
managing Windows software for large
spare room of Sumir's flat in Ealing,

ommune thrived. Microsoft became
and through the firm they obtained
panies such as NatWest and Barclays.
ever, the work dried up and, lacking
perience, they had no idea how to

forums for people running businesses from home. Twitter
is probably my biggest lifeline into the business community.
Whenever I need some help with how to do something, I
can just ask someone. It is lovely because people can just
go online and say they are feeling low and immediately
there will be four or five people saying, we are here, we are
listening, it's fine, don't worry, we have all been there. It
makes a big difference.'

I want to hold your hand

If you need general advice on setting up a business, check
out the Business Link website, businesslink.gov.uk, which
has practical advice on a wide range of subjects. One place
really worth visiting in person is the British Library's Business
and Intellectual Property Centre in London, bl.uk/bipc. The
people there can help you with business networking, business planning, researching markets and protecting your ideas
through courses, seminars and workshops.

If you need someone to guide you through your own
business, however, you need a mentor. A mentor is an experienced businessperson who has been there, done that,
whom you can meet or talk to on a regular, long-term basis,
who can provide wisdom and experience concerning the
week-by-week problems and issues you face. The best
mentoring relationship is one in which you are able to build
up a relationship of trust and understanding where both
sides feel they can speak freely and honestly with each other.
Because they are there over a long period they will be able
to see the progress you are making – and remind you of it

when you can't see it – and they will be able to help you put strategies into practice and be there to see them through.

A useful alternative is online mentoring, which is increasingly popular as it means you can do it from anywhere and it is a more informal arrangement. Several business support organisations now offer online mentoring, including Enterprise Nation, mentoring website Horsesmouth, and Shell Livewire, the advice organisation for young people. There is a full list on the Business Link website.

If you are under thirty, unemployed and without access to funding, get in touch with the Prince's Trust, which has for many years run a highly successful business-mentoring programme.

Trish Traynor-Watson, the founder of Liquid Space, a company which fits out offices, found a mentor in her former boss Gordon Bloor, who ran a property company. Having started up the business in 2003 with £20,000 of personal savings, her company has since grown to a turnover of £7 million. Trish credits her mentor's advice as having been key to her success, saying: 'When I worked for him I really learned how to run a business. I still speak to him every few weeks and we will sit up late into the night talking about the business and ideas. That has really helped.'

Indeed, it was during a conversation with Gordon that she came up with her most recent idea, the Office Lodger scheme, in which her firm helps clients find other companies willing to rent their unwanted office space.

Sometimes simply being able to talk through a problem and articulating what help you need can be enormously helpful. I recently called someone to ask for their help. While

I was breaking the help [...] able chunks to make it [...] was easy and wouldn't [...] the lines of, all you h[...] and fill in these four [...] the task was actually [...] initially thought and [...] time it would take [...]

If you find a me[...] completely differe[...] don't get on wit[...] relationship. Yo[...] the chemistry n[...] of working an[...] things in the [...]

Be specif[...]

Incidentall[...] for advice [...] right peo[...] The wor[...] who ha[...] and h[...] bad [...] from[...] you[...] the[...] th[...]

people. It is [...] than to bleed[...] wish they h[...] specific and [...] metaphorical[...] to guide you [...]

Consider it [...]

If you think yo[...] ad hoc advice, [...] professional adv[...] he started up his [...] computer error – [...] a sort of comm[...] colleagues.

Sumir, who grew [...] moved to the UK [...] says: 'The idea wa[...] technical experts i[...] company would be [...] The three of them [...] which specialised in [...] companies, from the [...] west London.

To start with, the [...] their biggest customer [...] work with other big com[...] After eight months, how[...] any kind of business ex[...]

162

160

fix the problem. So they sought help from Business Link and also asked a professional non-executive for advice.

The first thing the adviser told them was to ditch the commune idea and elect a leader. They chose Sumir. The second thing he said was that one of them had to go on a sales training course. Sumir offered to go.

He says of the adviser: 'He was frightfully expensive but gave us some of the best advice I've ever had in my life. In two to three sessions he got us to realign ourselves completely. We knew what we wanted to do but none of us had a clue how to run a business.' Two months later the newly structured team won a big contract with NPI, the insurer, and soon after that struck a big deal with Colt Telecom. Then, in 1999, Sumir wrote a programme that enabled organisations to turn on remotely all its computers when it needed to – and then remotely turn them all off again when it did not. The Nightwatchman programme transformed the fortunes of the business, which now has a turnover of more than £15 million. Sumir has since bought out his colleagues, realising he needed to run the business his own way.

Ruby Hammer and Millie Kendall, who created the Ruby & Millie make-up range for Boots, also decided to bring in an external adviser, Paul Kingsley, to help them with business strategy.

Their latest project is Scarlett & Crimson, a range of make-up for young girls inspired by cartoon characters, which is sold in Boots and Superdrug.

'Paul makes us function better,' says Ruby. 'He understands both of us and he brings something new to what we do without emotion. It has worked really well. A lot of owner-managers recruit people who replicate themselves but what is the point of that? It would be like talking to yourself. We don't want people who will go yes, yes, yes, because me and Millie can do that for each other.'

The very best way to find an adviser is through word-of-mouth recommendation from other small business owners or your industry trade association may be able to provide a list of contacts.

Consider the idea of a business partner

You may, on the other hand, decide that you need to bring in someone to help run your business on a more permanent basis. This is what Philip Weldon, the founder of The English Cheesecake Company, did. After leaving his job as an estate agent Philip started up his business in the kitchen of his flat making all the cheesecakes himself. Then he grew the business single-handedly for the next eighteen months, in that time moving production out of his home into an industrial unit and switching from chilled cheesecakes to selling frozen ones. By which time he had reached breaking point.

He says: 'I was waking up every morning knowing that nothing was going to be done unless I did it. It was very isolating and soul-destroying. I employed somebody but then I needed more staff and it was becoming a big strain. I had lost all my creativity and was spending too much time trouble-shooting.'

Philip had always been reluctant to take on a business partner, believing that if he chose the wrong person they might come in and 'rip the heart out of the business'. But, fortunately he managed to find, through a friend, someone who had recently sold a business of his own and was looking for a new challenge. Alan Laurier initially started working with Philip one day a week, but Philip quickly realised he was a perfect fit and so brought him in as a business partner. Alan immediately introduced tight operating controls and suggested that Philip increase his range of cheesecakes. Within a year, he had created more than a hundred flavours and had started making other cakes, too, such as chocolate fudge cake. Philip credits Alan with having transformed the business, which now has an annual turnover of £3 million.

Four years after Raoul Shah started his creative marketing agency Exposure, he too decided he needed to bring in outside help to make his business a success. So he invited a friend, Tim Bourne, to join him as an equal partner and gave him a 50 per cent stake. It was a bold step to take, giving a newcomer half of the entire business in the hope that he would help Raoul grow it further, but the gamble paid off. The firm, which is based in central London, now has a turnover of £20 million.

'People might say that was completely crazy,' says Raoul. 'However, it really fuelled the growth and here we are sixteen years on, having seen a lot of companies in our industry come and go. If I hadn't invested in key people over the years it would have been a smaller, less adventurous business.'

The crucial thing to remember in all of this is that, even though it might not feel like it at the time, you are not alone. There are thousands of fledgling entrepreneurs currently struggling with exactly the same problems and issues that you are grappling with.

And, just as importantly, there are thousands of entrepreneurs who were at that place once and who have now come through the other side to establish successful businesses. The chances are they are more than willing to pass on their expertise, so get in touch and ask for help. The worst they can do is say no, and their advice could just spell the difference for you between failure and success.

Finally, if you are fortunate enough to have someone offering to cook food for you, just say yes. In the early days of starting up a business you will probably not have enough time to wash or sleep, let alone cook for yourself. And living on takeaways is likely to get very tedious – and very unhealthy – very quickly.

ACTION PLAN

▶▶ Decide what kind of help you need. Do you need someone to help with a specific aspect of your business, or are you looking for someone to give you ongoing advice on a longer-term basis?

▶▶ Visit the British Library's Business and Intellectual Property Centre in London. At present it is the only one of its kind in the country and it is packed with resources. Before you go, check out the website at bl.uk/bipc and book a free one-to-one, hour-long session with one of their business or information experts.

▶▶ Write a list of people who may be able to help you. The ideal person will be someone who has worked in your industry but has now sold their business, so is likely to have the time and inclination to offer advice.

CHAPTER 14

GET OUT THERE AND PROMOTE YOURSELF

If you should bump into Graham Milton at a party the chances are that he will be wearing a tuxedo shirt with a flamboyant design on the back.

Graham started his business Fluxedo Shirts immediately after graduating from Nottingham University and since then he has seized every opportunity to show off his shirts. which look like traditional wing-collar shirts until the wearer removes his jacket to reveal the pattern on the back of the shirt. He has worn them in all kinds of unlikely places, such as the Notting Hill Carnival and music festivals where, as the only person in formal dress, he has really stood out from the crowd. As a result, whenever he goes anywhere in one of his shirts he get lots of people asking him about them and trying to find out where they can buy them.

Graham, who creates the designs himself and then gets them printed onto ready-made, plain white tuxedo shirts says: 'These days you have really got to think about your brand and about being the personality behind your brand. When you are a one-man band it makes sense to use yourself to promote your business.'

He's right. These days it is no good starting your business and then simply sitting back and hoping that somehow customers are going to find you and that sales are going to happen. You have to get out there and tell the world about your venture, and about yourself.

Opportunities are all around you

The good news is that, just as Graham is discovering, there are all sorts of simple but effective things you can do to get you and your products noticed. As the creator of your business and the person who knows most about it, you are already effectively the public face of that business – a walking, talking billboard, brand ambassador and roving representative all rolled into one. All you need to do now is realise that and make it work to your advantage.

Jane Robson has also spotted the potential for promoting her business, The Fine Cotton Company, which sells organic bed linen, cushions and throws, at every available opportunity. She uses her own products at her home in West Hampstead and as a result has often taken orders from friends when they visit her.

She says: 'When people come round they see nice cushions or throws and they can touch them and feel the quality. I will always tell people they are from my company. I have taken some orders over supper and can pop them through on the computer the next day. The business is such a major part of my life that I can never really switch off.'

Jane, who used to be a senior textiles buyer for Debenhams before starting up her business in 2008, says she is very aware of being an ambassador for her business. 'I am my business. I am always on show. When you work in a corporate environment you can go home in the evening and switch off. But I am always thinking about the business. I am always conscious I am the spokesperson and that it is my livelihood and that I need to make it work.'

Of course, the idea that you are the face of your business can be a pretty daunting one when you are having a bad hair day, or yelling at the kids or having an argument with a traffic warden.

And it might be the last thing you want to think about as you're helping yourself to another glass of wine at a party. Whereas people with jobs can switch off from them when they leave the office, your business, because it is part of you, goes with you everywhere.

Dancing on the table to 'The Winner Takes It All' in front of a group of potential customers is probably never going to be a good idea. But being 'always on' can lead to some amazing opportunities to do business in the most unlikely places. Every conversation and every chance meeting, whether in the supermarket, on a train or at the swimming pool, offers an opportunity to build sales and new relationships.

Ali Wallace, who started up his own recruitment agency, DNA, has also discovered that being 'always on' can reap enormous benefits. Ali has found several new clients simply by chatting to fellow commuters on the train from his home in north Hertfordshire to London.

Ali says: 'I have always been a naturally outgoing, sociable person. When I started commuting I thought it would be a living hell but you end up meeting a lot of people on the train. My first piece of business came through meeting someone on the train who knew someone else and I have had three or four successful pieces of business purely through meeting people on train journeys and connecting people with each other.'

In your enthusiasm to promote your business, however, you do have to be careful not to overstep the line and turn into the equivalent of that annoying insurance salesman who keeps accosting Bill Murray in the film *Groundhog Day*.

This is something that Ali has always been particularly conscious about avoiding. He says: 'I am my business and I am always on but I am very cautious not to come across as someone who goes on about his business. It is about always taking advantage of any opportunity you find yourself in, but in an appropriate fashion. Being successful is not about ramming anything down anybody's throat. It is about understanding people and getting to know them first. I am at work from the minute I get out of bed to the minute I get back into bed.'

So how do you make the most of this incredible opportunity? The secret is to realise that every kind of occasion, whether planned or unexpected, represents an opportunity for an entrepreneur to do business. And then be prepared. Before you attend a business event, for example, ask the organisers in advance for a guest list of who is going to be there and what they do, so that if the opportunity arises you can introduce yourself. There is nothing more infuriating than realising that the head buyer for Homebase, for example, was at a networking drinks party but you weren't aware of it.

And whenever you go on a flight anywhere, whether for business or pleasure, introduce yourself to the person sitting next to you and find out what they do. You never know who it might be. If they turn out to be a crashing bore, you can always plug yourself into the in-flight entertainment system for the rest of the trip.

Beware, however, of not breaching the etiquette of the occasion – there is no faster way of putting people off you and your business than blatantly trying to promote it at inappropriate social occasions. If you discover that someone you want to meet is at your godson's christening by all means introduce yourself, but wait until after the event to send an email inviting further discussion.

Even if no immediate opportunity to do business presents itself, it is worth staying in touch with the people you have met, by sending them an email after the event and even introducing them to other people who may be useful to them, in order to keep the contact alive. That way they are more likely to remember you when something comes along that would be relevant to your business.

Being 'always on' also means that you need to be prepared for a chance encounter. Obviously always carry business cards, but, even better, carry or wear some samples of your products and perhaps have an information pack ready to give to someone, too. And kit yourself out with a BlackBerry or iPhone so you can instantly send and receive emails instead of waiting until you get back to the office, when you will probably have forgotten about it. I spoke at a conference for entrepreneurs recently where I gave out my email address and welcomed anyone with an interesting story to tell to get in touch: by the time I was on the train home I had already received six emails. It's simple but it impresses people – it certainly impressed me – and it makes them remember you.

Put on your smiley face – first impressions do count

You also need to be very careful who you chat freely to about your business: you never know who they might turn out to be. If your business is not doing well, keep it to yourself because that stranger you are confiding in could well be a customer, or supplier, or potential investor, or even someone who works at the bank where your account is held.

Unfortunately, if a business is in trouble it can become toxic very quickly. Other people become reluctant to do business with you because they are worried that they will not get the products they requested, or that they will lose money. Or even that their business will become tainted by association if your business folds. So smile and be positive at all times and save the gloom for when you are at home or truly alone.

The fact is, the way you talk about your business can make all the difference in the world to how other people see it and therefore ultimately how successful it is likely to be. I was at another conference not long ago giving a speech to an audience of small business owners, many of whom had only recently set up their businesses. After I had finished speaking lots of people came up to me to thrust business cards into my hand and to tell me enthusiastically about their ventures, whether they were making jewellery or selling clothes or even holiday homes. They were all clearly so excited to be able to throw their energy into something they loved doing and were thrilled to have been able to take the plunge and follow their dream. Whatever the actual prospects for their business, it was evident that lack of enthusiasm and drive was not going to be a problem.

Then, after I had finished talking to them, I noticed a lady who had not come up to talk to me so I asked her whether she had a business, not really expecting her to say yes. But she did have a business, and after a bit of probing she told me what she did, and it all sounded very interesting, if perhaps a fairly specialised product to try and sell. I found myself wondering if she shouldn't perhaps be trying a different approach to win new customers. But what really shouted volumes about her business was the flat, listless way she talked about it. She had an air of total defeat about her. Her eyes looked weary, her mouth looked sad and her shoulders drooped. Every part of her indicated that she had given up on this business, and found it too hard, and had no motivation or enthusiasm for it any longer. If I had been a potential customer her dejected air would have completely put me off looking at her website, let alone buying anything and – worse – if I had been a potential investor I would have run a mile. And all because of what this lady revealed about herself and her business in a five-minute conversation. It may be shallow and trite, but the fact is that first impressions do count and you have got to make sure that yours are counting for the right reasons.

Think creatively

So, apart from talking to people at parties and trying to create a great impression, what else can you do to promote your business out there in the big wide world? The answer is a lot.

At first glance the idea of promotion sounds as if it is going to cost a lot of money, but there are some very simple yet effective things you can do to promote your business. Your first step should be to get in touch with your local newspaper and tell them about your business. If they find it interesting, they might write a story about you. Are you just about to open a new factory and create lots of local jobs? Have you just launched a product made from local ingredients? Are you doing something out of the ordinary? 'Small Lancashire firm supplies NASA with space food', for example, would be an amazing story, if that is what you do. 'Newcastle firm wins national award for innovation' is another good one.

Not only is coverage like this free, it will also give your business and product far greater credibility than a paid-for advert could ever achieve. I know what I am talking about – there is a reason why I am constantly bombarded with emails and phone calls from public relations people asking if I would write about their clients in my 'How I Made It' column, or as part of a feature, and I know it is not because they are simply trying to be friendly and helpful. The impact of being written about in the small business pages of *The Sunday Times* compared to simply taking out an advert is enormous, not just in terms of the number of people who will see it and read it, but in terms of how seriously people will regard it.

And before you ask, yes, if you too have a good story to tell, then I would be delighted to hear it. You can email me via my website, rachelbridge.com.

On the subject of national awards, I suggest that as soon as your business is established, you enter it for as many local and national business awards as you can. There seems to be a new 'Entrepreneur of the Year' competition popping up every week – someone has to win them and if you are creating something special it might as well be you. If you are shortlisted as a runner-up, or, even better, if you win, you will get lots of press coverage and recognition which is a truly fabulous way of promoting your business.

Be a case study

Something else you can do is make yourself known to the big businesses whose services you use and see if they might want to use you as a case study. You may not know this but the Post Office, for example, or your bank, or even your broadband provider are always being asked by journalists if they have business customers willing to talk to them. So see if they might want to talk to you. It is free and so long as you are not talking about anything controversial which could offend potential customers, it will be good exposure for your business, too.

If you join a small business organisation such as the Federation of Small Businesses, or the Forum of Private Business, or your local Chambers of Commerce, tell them you would be happy to be a case study too. Journalists like me are always looking for interesting small firms to talk to about a particular subject and include in a feature – it could be anything from business rates and the budget to the joys of working with animals, or what it's like to work from home. And you might even get your photo included with the piece as well.

Once you start thinking about this, there are truly loads of things you can do to get your name in front of potential customers. You could sponsor the local cricket team. You could get together with other local businesses to promote your town as a food destination, or holiday destination, or dinosaur-finding destination. You could even paint your car with your company logo and put your phone number and website on it. (It is probably wisest to involve a professional in this rather than simply launching yourself at it with spray can in hand. Also, make sure it is legible. I saw a painted car the other day but the name on it was so arty and creative that I practically had to drive into the rear bumper to be able to read it.)

In fact, you should always put your phone number and website on anything and everything you can. If you are a party planner and provide staff to take part in external events then get them to wear T-shirts with your logo and phone and website details on the back.

When Asher Moses started his business Taxi Promotions, offering advertising space on the side of his fleet of taxis, he began by using his vehicles to promote tourism in America by decorating fifty cabs in the style of the fifty US states, after selling the idea to the Visit USA organisation.

Asher then decided that adverts on his taxis would work well for First Direct, the telephone bank, which had just been launched. When the person at the bank responsible for making these kinds of decisions refused to arrange a meeting, Moses simply went ahead and painted one of his cabs in the First Direct colours and style. Then he fitted it out with a phone that connected straight to First Direct and drove it to the bank's head office. The director he had been trying to get in contact with came straight down to see the extraordinary looking taxi parked outside and immediately sat in the back and used the phone. He loved the idea, says Asher, and most of the rest of the bank came down to look at the taxi as well. The deal ultimately fell through because Asher did not have enough of a trading history to meet the bank's strict criteria, but it was certainly not for want of trying. And Asher's business has gone from strength to strength. It now has the rights to advertise on 1,600 taxis and has a turnover of £3 million.

The other simple but effective way to promote your business is to make your website address the same as the name of your business, plus the .com or .co.uk ending. In other words, if your business is called Blue Whale, then your website should be bluewhale.com, or bluewhale.co.uk. That way, people will be able to find your website simply by knowing your business name. And if a search engine does not throw up the right result then a potential customer will still be able to find you by guessing the website address.

It sounds blindingly obvious but it is amazing how many people don't think to do this. B&Q's website, for example, is diy.com, which might have seemed like a brilliant idea in the days before internet search engines such as Google were invented, but is less so now. And British Gas's website, as displayed on the back of their vans, is house.co.uk. Not at all obvious why that might once have been thought a good idea. Wisely, they have since added britishgas.co.uk, which leads to the same place.

Don't worry if making your business name your domain name makes your website address seem quite long as a result. These days, people are much more comfortable than they were with typing in a long business name into their search engine, as notonthehighstreet.com, iwantoneofthose.com and dosomethingdifferent.com have all discovered. What they suffer in unwieldiness they make up for in impact and memorability.

ACTION PLAN

▶▶ Draw up a list of local newspapers and trade magazines, both print and online, which might be interested in writing about your company. Find out which journalists write about your sector – by identifying their byline or ringing the switchboard – then send an email introducing yourself. Remember to keep it short and to the point.

▶▶ Write a list of events that you would like your firm to be associated with. Then get in touch with the organisers and find out how to do this. Your local council website, for example, will have details of annual fairs, farmers' markets, town hall events and so on.

▶▶ Align your business name and your website domain name. Then put your website address and phone number on everything you can think of.

CHAPTER 15

LOVE (MOST OF) YOUR CUSTOMERS

Andrew Stanley's first attempt at organising a golfing holiday was nearly his last. He had arranged a Ryder Cup-style event for a group of twenty-four people in a hotel in Le Touquet, northern France, over a weekend. Unfortunately, on the first night two of the golfers had a punch-up in the hotel bar after having too much to drink. The incident did not go down well with the hotel management.

Andrew says: 'On my return to England on the Monday morning I received a fax from the hotel and golf course cancelling my contract because they didn't want that kind of business.'

In a panic at losing his only supplier, Andrew went straight back to Le Touquet to try to persuade the hotel manager to change his mind.

'I pleaded for them to give me a second chance and promised it wouldn't happen again,' he says. Fortunately for him they agreed and his golfing holiday business, golf-breaks.com, has since grown to a turnover of £20 million.

Sometimes it can seem as if you could run your company a lot more smoothly if you didn't actually have to get any customers involved. Just when you have got everything all carefully planned, along come your customers and mess things up.

Andrew Valentine and Brett Akker had the same problem. When they started up Streetcar, their car-sharing club, they promised customers a twenty-four-hour customer care service. Lovely idea, but in the early days they could not afford to employ a call centre to help them. Which meant that Andrew and Brett would often be answering calls from potential customers at all hours of the day and night.

Andrew says: 'We would get a prospective member ringing up at 3 a.m. having just seen a flyer, asking for more information about how Streetcar worked. We were determined enough to still do a great sales job but it was pretty tough going.'

All customers are not created equal

Without customers, of course, you wouldn't actually have a business so it pays to try to be nice to them, even if it is sometimes through gritted teeth. But all customers are not created equal and sometimes customers really are more trouble than they are worth. And those are the ones you need to get rid of. Fast.

Now when you are starting up a business it can seem unthinkable to start getting rid of customers when surely what you are trying to do is to get as many of them as you can. Well, yes and no. The wrong sort of customers can not only sap your energy as you spend all your time trying to please them and attend to their every need; they can actually do irreparable harm to your company by diverting your attention away from the good customers who might have been willing to spend a lot more money with you if only you hadn't been so preoccupied elsewhere.

Ironically, it is often the very customers you tried so hard to get – the big, prestigious, corporate ones – that are the ones you need to get rid of. While on the face of it they might be spending large sums of money with your company, the chances are that the profit margins you are getting on that business are very slim because the big customer is likely to have pared your prices to the core during negotiations. Partly because the sheer volume of work they were offering you was so big, partly because they were a lot better at the negotiating game than you. Ask yourself, is the gain really worth the pain? It could be that the amount of time you have to spend servicing their needs is simply not worth it compared to the profit you get from doing business with them.

And if they are not making money for you, then you have to be brutal. Never forget it is profit, not turnover, that counts in this game. Yes, they may be big and prestigious but as a small firm – indeed, as a firm of any size – you cannot afford to carry customers who are not contributing as much to your bottom line as they are taking up valuable management resources.

Indeed, losing one of your bigger clients could actually turn out to be a worthwhile sacrifice, because it frees up capacity which allows you to win lots of smaller but better clients at better profit margins. And if you do win new clients then that in itself has a halo effect, because your existing clients will take notice and it will help them justify to themselves why they are staying with you.

John Griffin is the founder of Addison Lee, the highly successful minicab firm which has an annual turnover of £180 million. He has long followed the policy of going for lots of smaller customers rather than a handful of large corporate customers for this very reason.

He says: 'I don't want big accounts. I want loads and loads of accounts. We have got 15,000 accounts and that to me is fine. I have never really gone after big accounts.'

The one time he did have a big, prestigious corporate customer, he says, the firm made such unreasonable demands and put him under such a lot of pressure that he decided he didn't want to continue working with them any more.

Welcome the complaints

Even your nice, fat-margin customers are occasionally going to demand your time and attention, of course. One of the unavoidable problems of running your own business is having to deal with the odd disgruntled customer. You should be pleased about this, though – the odd complaint can actually be really useful as it is effectively a free piece of market research which is telling you what is wrong with what you are doing. So if you have done something wrong, you should count yourself lucky that they have come to you to make a complaint – and thereby give you a chance to fix it – rather than simply gone off and told all their friends what a terrible company you are. Or, worse, put their complaint online where the rest of the world would see it.

A few years ago Stena Line, which runs ferries between Scotland and Ireland carrying 17.3 million passengers a year, decided to take a radical approach to dealing with complaining customers. It gave all five hundred of its employees the power to give away up to £1,000 on the spot to compensate customers who were not happy with the service they received.

Alan Gordon, a spokesman for the company, says: 'We now work on a system of "fix it plus one" – if a meal is cold, for example, we will replace the meal and also give dessert. We respond to all correspondence from customers within two days, and if it is something particularly bad then we will phone them. As a result, the whole culture of the company has changed. In 1999 we had four complaints for every one compliment that we received. Now we get one compliment for every complaint.'

But what if you get stuck with the customer from hell who complains endlessly about everything your company does and has made it their mission to make your life a misery? You first need to understand why they are being difficult, because if they have a genuine complaint then dealing with it could be an opportunity to strengthen your relationship with them. If it is simply because they like complaining, however, then you have to get rid of them. You have two options. You could simply say to the customer that you are sorry but you don't want to work with them any more. Or you could tell them you are going to have to double your fees to provide the kind of service they require. After all, if they are prepared to pay double and the profit margin is good, you might just be able to tolerate them.

How to hold on to the nice ones

So you've got your band of happy customers and they are all contributing nicely to your profits. What next? Well, first you need to hold on to them. And then you need to find more customers just like them. And you need to do it in that order, something many first-time entrepreneurs forget. It is eight times cheaper to hold on to an existing customer than it is to go out and find a new one, because the first lot are already on your side.

The rewards for creating a loyal customer base are immense, not just in terms of profits, but in terms of the satisfaction you get when something is working well.

When customers of Architectural Plants in Horsham, Sussex, receive the invoice for their order they also get a small envelope containing two silver balloons and a piece of string. The label on the envelope reads: 'A slightly strange and really rather selfish request: this envelope contains a couple of silver balloons and some string. If you could bear to blow them up and hang them outside your house as close to the road as possible, it would make life wonderfully simple for our driver who will be looking for your house to deliver your plant. Many thanks.'

It is a small thing, but, according to Angus White, the

founder of Architectural Plants, it has paid dividends. Customers get their deliveries on time and they know that the company they are buying from cares that they do. 'I would say that 99 per cent of people do it. It is really nice,' he says.

The balloons are just one way in which Architectural Plants has gone the extra mile to please its customers. Inside the store are comfy sofas and customers can help themselves to free coffee and biscuits while they think about what they want to buy.

Angus says the whole thrust of the company's policy was to treat customers as equals. 'Even if somebody phones up to complain, I try to make it clear that I am not interested in having an "indignant customer, defensive shopkeeper" type of conversation. It is pointless. I tell them we are going to have an intelligent conversation and find a solution to the problem. If you underestimate customers' intelligence, you are in trouble.'

Customer service is like a stone dropped into a pond. When it is done well the effects spread far and wide. When it is done badly exactly the same thing happens.

Ian Wellens is another small business owner who has built up a lovely relationship with his customers. Ian founded his cheese company The Cheese Shed in 2006 and now sells more than a hundred handmade artisan cheeses from the West Country, made mainly by small producers.

Whenever Ian makes one of his renowned wedding cheeses, made from several large, round cheeses assembled to look like a wedding cake, he is often delighted to receive a photograph of the occasion a few weeks later.

Ian says: 'People feel they have a relationship with me. It

is not just about being a Cheese Shed customer, it is about being a customer of me. There must be something invested in our relationship otherwise they wouldn't bother.'

For Ian the personal touch has always been an intrinsic part of his approach, despite the fact that his is essentially an internet-based business. He always, for example, sends customers the story behind the cheese they buy and details of the people who make it.

He says: 'I think having a genuine commitment and enthusiasm for what you are selling will always count. In these straitened times there is still going to be a space for those things that people think add a bit of excitement and value and quality to their lives.'

Think local

So how you do you go about getting yourself a loyal customer base? One way is to concentrate on creating a strong following in your local area. That is what Will Gemmel has done in south-west London, where his distinctive Affleck Property Services vans parked on the street are a highly visible advertisement for his business. In reality, his firm, which provides property maintenance and building services, has only eight vans but because they are distinctive and operate in a small area, it gives the impression that there are dozens of them whizzing around.

Being so visible in a small area can reap huge dividends, Will says. 'We have built up a strong reputation in this area because people like what we do and recommend us to their neighbours. When you are a local firm you cannot get away with poor-quality work otherwise you would soon go out of business.'

Will is well aware that every job the firm does has the potential either to enhance or damage its reputation. 'We put up signs outside each job with our name and number on and we post flyers in every house on the street at the end of each job to build brand awareness,' he says. 'We want people to see us and to say, that is who did my house. We are not just here to make some money and then go away. We are here for the long term.'

There are also cost advantages to being local. 'It means our project managers can manage more jobs at the same time without the quality being reduced,' he says. 'If we had jobs in north and south London, for example, it would be impossible for them to manage both.'

Another option is to create a loyal virtual community online, where customers feel they are part of something that values and appreciates their input. This is what online retail giant Amazon does, by letting customers write reviews of all its products, and, most importantly, by letting them create online virtual lists of their favourite books which they can then share with other Amazon users through the website.

Remember, customers like to be appreciated and listened to. So talk to them, listen to their plans, their concerns, their hopes and fears, go and see them, invite them to things, send them newspaper articles you think they might be interested in. They will love you for it. One of the most common reasons for customers not coming back is that they don't feel they were looked after as much as they should have been.

And remember that it is not a one-way street. Talking to your customers can be a fantastic way of finding out not only what you are doing well and where you could be doing better, but also what your rivals are up to. They have a huge amount of market information and intelligence, which you need to know.

But make sure they pay you

The most important thing about customers, however, is that you need to make sure they actually pay you. The number of business customers paying late or not at all has soared over the past couple of years due to the difficult economic climate, leaving small firms horribly exposed to bad debts and many pushed over the edge into insolvency through no fault of their own.

Insolvency experts estimate that about 80 per cent of businesses which lose a big customer do not survive. According to the Federation of Small Businesses, about 10 per cent of the small firms that fail do so because a customer has not been able to pay its bills. The problem has been made worse because small firms are finding it increasingly difficult to get credit insurance – which pays out if customers don't – leaving them completely exposed if something goes wrong.

Fortunately, there is something you can do about it. Whenever you take on customers who are paying you in arrears after they have already received your goods and services – say thirty or sixty days after the invoice is sent out, as most trade customers do – make sure you run a credit check on them first. A lot of small businesses will still take on customers on trust, because they know the owner, for example, or because they have done business with the firm before. Or because, in the early days of running a company, they don't feel that they can turn customers down. YOU MUST NOT DO THIS. The economic downturn and credit crunch has changed all that. Your customers' credit problems will quickly become your problems if they don't pay you, which means it is imperative that you run a credit check on every trade customer before you supply them, and turn away customers whose numbers do not stack up.

And don't just do it once. Credit-check them continually because their financial circumstances can change from week to week – as, indeed, will yours if they are suddenly unable to pay you. In order to run a credit check on a new or potential customer, either ask them to supply you with a credit check report themselves or else you can download a copy yourself online from a credit checking agency such as Experian or Equifax at a small cost. You should also ask your potential customer for a copy of both their latest filed accounts and their up-to-date management accounts. These are the internal book-keeping records that show the profit and loss, balance sheet and other trading information. The information should have been updated within the last month. Ask them, too, for details of at least two trade references of existing trade customers or suppliers that you can call.

Alternatively, several high street banks now offer free or inexpensive credit checking services for customers so ask yours what it can offer you.

Remember, an order that is not paid for is not business,

it is a bad debt and a drain on your company's finances. And make sure you send out watertight terms and conditions with every order, including a retention clause in their terms and conditions, which means that, if you provide various items of stock to a firm that then becomes insolvent, you retain title of ownership over those goods. You should also keep very tight control over all unpaid invoices; call your customers a few days before payment is due to remind them politely that it is about to become due so they can start processing it. Then call them again the moment any payments become overdue and remind them, again politely, that they need to pay immediately. And continue to chase the payment until you receive it. Don't rely on sending passive reminders such as letters or emails, as they frequently get overlooked and are easy to ignore. It is much harder to ignore a phone call. You might find it daunting to call a customer you know well and ask to be paid, but, remember, your firm's future may depend on it. You know it makes sense.

ACTION PLAN

▶▶ Construct a proper database of your customers and how often they place orders and of what size, and update it regularly.

▶▶ Don't agree to customers' demands just because they are big. Make sure it makes sense for your business as well as theirs.

▶▶ Carry out regular credit checks on all the customers you supply. And don't feel bad about turning work away if you think the customer is not going to be able to pay. Business is no place to be sentimental.

CHAPTER 16

SEIZE THOSE OPPORTUNITIES

Burts Chips, a small firm based in Devon, was all set to launch its hand-fried potato crisps in Holland when its Dutch distributor suddenly pointed out that the range did not include a paprika-flavoured crisp. It was a serious omission – paprika is by far the most popular flavour of crisp in Holland and the firm would have been at a considerable commercial disadvantage without it.

With no time to lose, the firm's co-owners Jonty White and Nick Hurst immediately abandoned everything else they were doing and got to work creating a paprika-flavoured crisp plus the packaging to put it in.

Jonty says: 'We had to seriously pull the stops out. I did the design work very quickly and then we spent two days with our flavour people working through the ingredients together.'

In the end it took just three weeks for them to create and package a paprika crisp for the Dutch market. It was launched there in 2009 and was such an outstanding success that a few months later Burts launched their paprika-flavoured crisps in the UK as well.

Says Jonty: 'That's the joy of running a small business; you can just get your team together and work things through very quickly. We didn't have to go through focus groups or have long committee meetings, we just said, yes, let's do it. It would have taken a big company at least six months to launch a new product like this.'

When you are starting up a new venture you have one fantastically useful advantage over your larger, more established competitors – you can be extremely nimble on your feet. You don't have the baggage of a corporate structure, you don't have the limitations of a team of staff who are set in their ways, or people around you who tut and say things like, oh, but we don't do things like that around here. Instead, you, the agile entrepreneur, can make instant decisions instead of having to put them to a committee, and you can direct money and resources to projects without having to ask anyone's permission. That means that if you spot a money-making opportunity you really can move fast to grab it before it gets away. That is very exciting and very liberating and you should do everything you can to make the most of it.

It is something that big, established companies long to be able to do, and never really can, no matter how hard they try, because corporate baggage is hard to get rid of and because, just like being middle-aged, you can never go back to the days when you were young and carefree. Luckily for you, that is where you and your new business are at right now. Hooray.

Seize the day

Opportunities don't have to be complicated. It could be something as simple as reacting to the weather. I love it when street traders suddenly appear with a sackful of cheap umbrellas to sell when it's pouring with rain, or when the bar round the corner from my house puts a sign up advertising mulled wine by the glass when the weather suddenly turns cold. Or when supermarkets put out big displays of disposal barbecues, beer and ready-to-cook kebabs the moment the sun starts to shine.

Sometimes an opportunity to do business might arise because of what is happening in your market. Ryanair often leaps into action with adverts in newspapers offering special flight promotions when BA, one of its competitors, is threatened by strike action. On a more local level, if all the cafés around you are charging people to use Wi-Fi, then why not offer it for free? That's the café I'm choosing to sit in right now, having deliberately walked straight past another equally nice café, but one which would like to charge me an outrageous £5.99 for ninety minutes of Wi-Fi activity. No thanks.

It is even easier to move fast when your venture is entirely online. All you have to do is redo the home page to highlight your offer. Want to advertise the fact that you use a courier service so your deliveries will not be affected by a postal strike, unlike those of your competitors? Or to hold a one-day-only clearance sale of selected products? A few moments' typing and it's done.

It drives me mad when businesses don't seize the opportunity to move fast and react to changing events. It constantly amazes me that shops switch to selling spring and summer clothes in mid-January, even though it is clearly still winter outside and about minus three degrees and no one actually wants to buy shorts and cotton dresses. I've lost count of the number of times I have gone into a shop and tried to buy a hat, or a pair of gloves, or a pair of boots, only to be told by a sales assistant in a shocked voice, oh no, madam, we stopped stocking our winter season weeks ago. But it's snowing outside! I'm freezing! Why aren't you selling scarves instead of hiding them away in your warehouse? Surely there is room for both on the shop floor for a changeover period? And then I sigh deeply as yet another business falls victim to the old 'but we don't do it like that round here' line. So easy, and yet so hard to do, for some reason.

Then there is the pub we went to the other day that refused to serve my sister a full English breakfast even though it was on the menu because, the waitress told us, 'the chef has already put the bacon away'. Er, hello, you have a potential paying customer here; get the bacon out of the fridge.

Happily, some small companies have discovered the value of the opportunity they have been given. Not long ago, Jane Field, the founder of a firm called Jonny's Sister, which makes bespoke bunting and cushions, received a call from a man who wanted to order bunting which read 'Will you marry me?' so that he could propose to his girlfriend while they were on holiday. The catch was that he and his girlfriend were leaving in two days' time. Undaunted, Jane and her team got to work – and when they realised that a courier could not deliver before the customer left for his flight, Jane drove from Yeovil to Bristol airport and handed over the bunting herself.

As she rightly says: 'If we had been a big company it just wouldn't have happened. The order would probably have had to go through several hoops before it went into production and it certainly wouldn't have got to Bristol airport on time. We work all hours and we get excited by challenges. So far there has not been one request we have not been able to handle.'

Learn the art of thinking on your feet

As a first-time entrepreneur without the baggage of a big corporate structure, your ability to move fast gives you an incredible advantage over your bigger competitors, and you should never forget it. You and your larger rival might both spot the same opportunities, but whereas your corporate competitor will have to start organising meetings and drawing up strategic plans and all manner of stuff before they are actually able to do anything about it, you can jump straight in, modifying or enhancing or even reversing the activities of your firm to take advantage of new opportunities – all within the space of an afternoon, if need be. Which means that you can beat the competition to it by days, weeks, even months.

James Minter is the owner of Adam Street private members' club and recently started running the bar and restaurant at The Tabernacle in Notting Hill, west London, which is situated right in the middle of the area where the Notting Hill Carnival takes place every August. The first year James decided to charge a £5 entrance fee to allow people to sit in the garden and escape the crowds. It quickly became apparent, however, that not many people were interested in paying to get in. So after a few hours James scrapped that idea and allowed everyone in, making money by selling Caribbean food at the bar.

However, this plan, too, had its flaws as James soon discovered the venue was attracting a large number of people who simply wanted to use the lavatory. Let me tell you, there is always an acute shortage of toilets during the carnival.

So James had another rethink and, because he only had himself to consult, he immediately started charging non-eating customers £1 to use the lavatory.

The reworked plan was a huge success both in terms of making money and keeping numbers manageable and James now plans to repeat it next year. He says: 'It was really important to be able to move quickly and I could do that because I was on the spot making decisions on an hour-by-hour basis.'

Be flexible

So, how do you, the first-time entrepreneur, make the most of this amazing super-power you have been granted – the ability to move fast and make quick decisions?

First, be flexible and keep an open mind. Being able to move fast is as much about having the right state of mind as anything else. And get used to making instant decisions and acting on them. Whatever you do, don't put off making any kind of decision at all. That will just leave you and your business in a state of paralysis, unable to move forward or back.

Then make sure you are completely tuned in to your market so you know what is happening, what is about to happen and where new opportunities are likely to spring from. Talk to your customers, go to where they hang out and hang out there too, whether that be a conference or a café on the beach. Keep your ear to the ground, pick up gossip.

Opportunities can occur when you least expect them. Sylvia Tidy Harris was busy taking bookings for her public-speaking agency The Speakers Agency when she suddenly realised she had far fewer women than men on her books, and yet there were a lot of talented women who were experts in their fields, who she thought would make brilliant speakers.

So she trawled through possible website domain names and when she found that womenspeakers.co.uk was still available she knew it was too good an opportunity to miss.

Her Women Speakers' website was launched in 2004 and now represents four hundred high-profile women. They include the singer Toyah Wilcox, television presenter Amanda Lamb and the former MP Edwina Currie. Clients can book them to speak at dinners, conferences and events.

'When I first had the idea I was astounded that nobody else had already thought of it,' she says. 'I have had an enormous amount of interest from companies looking for women speakers and I have had a huge amount of enthusiasm and support from women I asked to join the agency. Since the agency was launched we have taken as many bookings as we did for my original speakers' agency. I knew that without innovation any business is going to become stagnant. You just can't rest on your laurels and wait for something good to come along. You have to do something to make sure this happens.'

Before leaping into new things at random, however, you need to do two things:

▶▶ Make sure whatever you are doing is in line with your strategy for your business and fits in with what you are already doing. Sylvia's idea for her women-only speaking agency, for example, was a perfect match for the speaking agency she already had, and indeed was really simply a way of adding an extra facet and marketing peg.

▶▶ Decide whether the opportunity you have spotted is likely to be a short-lived phenomenon. If it looks like a short-term fad, you can still make money, but as a first-time entrepreneur you need to tread very carefully indeed. Fads and trends can disappear as quickly as they arrived, leaving you wrong-footed and, at best, with a lot of unwanted stock on your hands; at worst, without a business at all. To start with, when the things are selling well, it may seem like easy money, but when the trend ends – which is likely to be as quickly as it began – then you could find yourself with a lot of unwanted stock. Remember Tamagotchi, or shag pile carpet, or puffball skirts?

All once huge, all now long since gone. Someone somewhere made a lot of money from selling them – and someone else still has a warehouse full of them, gathering dust.

Russell Ambrose, an entrepreneur who went on to set up Optimax, a firm offering laser eye treatment, found this out the hard way. His father owned several gift shops along the Essex seafront and as a child he would often help out during the school holidays. After getting a business degree at Leeds University, he decided to go into business himself. He spent the summer working in his father's shop at Jaywick Sands and noticed a man on the piece of land next to the shop selling 'clackers', a toy made from two balls on a piece of string. Ambrose saw how much money the man was making and so one evening he followed him and found out where he was buying the clackers.

Russell bought some for himself and the next day started selling them in the same place. At the end of the week, however, the man who had been there first bought all the clackers from the supplier, leaving Russell empty-handed. Undaunted, he simply found himself a firm that made plastic moulds and started making clackers himself

Initially it was easy money. He says: 'They cost me a few pence to make and I was selling them for 10 shillings [50p] each.' But after four months it all turned sour. The *Daily Mirror* ran a series of articles warning about the dangers of clackers, which it claimed were causing injuries. Suddenly nobody wanted to buy them any more and Russell was left with 100,000 pairs of clackers he could not sell. He says: 'The craze literally died over that weekend. It ran for three months and then it was all over.' He held on to the unsold clackers for several months but when it was clear that the craze was not coming back he had to throw them away, losing a lot of money in the process.

Knowing when to leave a market is just as import-ant as knowing when to dive in. Look at Blockbuster. Ten years ago, before the advent of the DVD, satellite and cable tele-vision, Blockbuster video stores were the kings of the high street. There was one in every neighbourhood and for many people they were an intrinsic part of the weekend. Everyone went to Blockbuster. But now technology has moved on leaving Blockbuster looking like a curious relic from the past – and laden with debt, with the US parent company warning in early 2010 that it might have to file for bankruptcy.

Don't get set in your ways

Sometimes you might find that being flexible involves more than writing a new home page or putting some barbecues on display.

Gary Frank, for example, discovered that the opportunity he thought he had spotted was not the one that was to make his fortune. When he lost his job in the City trading futures on the stock market and started up a business, he thought he was going to be selling doughnuts. In fact, he even had a dream about it, in which an old man was telling him to make doughnuts. He wrote a business plan and, having no money of his own, raised £30,000, borrowing £15,000 from family and friends and £15,000 from the bank. Then he hired an industrial unit near Oxford and started making American-style ring doughnuts, calling his venture The Delicious Donut Company. He would start making the doughnuts at midnight and then drive to Oxford or London at five o'clock in the morning to deliver them to sandwich bars and delicatessens, returning home mid-afternoon to catch up on paperwork and try to get a bit of sleep.

Unfortunately, after a year of doing this he, not surprisingly, became ill. Even more disheartening, despite having achieved sales of £45,000, he made a loss of £15,000 in his first year. So Gary started buying in other products such as flapjacks and muffins to sell alongside his doughnuts. They sold much better than the doughnuts, and in the second year Gary had sales of £250,000 and made a profit. For the next four years sales continued to grow – but not sales of his doughnuts. Demand was so poor that by 1995 he realised there was no point in continuing to hammer away with his doughnuts. So he stopped selling them altogether.

By this time his brother had joined the company and so they started making all the flapjacks and muffins themselves. There was just one small problem. The firm's original name, The Delicious Donut Company, was clearly not going to work any more, so in 1997 the Franks renamed it The Fabulous Bakin' Boys. The firm now employs 130 people and has sales of £12.5 million a year.

In order to be able to respond quickly to changing situations, you need to make sure you have the back-up and resources to enable you to see your decision through.

Establish good working relationships with your suppliers so they will be happy to change direction mid-flow if need be. You can do this by talking to them on a regular basis – about where the business is heading and how that will involve them. Be efficient and professional when dealing with them. And, most importantly, always pay them on time.

Make sure you keep any shareholders in the loop, too. Even if they are only your parents and friends, make regular semi-formal presentations to them about how the business is going.

Finally, remember that the best opportunities are not always the most obvious ones. The 2012 London Olympics will soon be upon us and I am sure that a stack of firms both large and small are already preparing for the Games, with Olympics-related products and services and promotions and souvenirs. Which is all very fine and lovely, but with such a high-profile event there will also be lots of competition, and no real way of estimating demand. I am willing to bet that when the Olympics extravaganza eventually rolls out of town there will be an awful lot of small businesses with unwanted souvenir mugs. The best opportunities are always the ones you spot yourself.

ACTION PLAN

▶▶ Take a look at what your competitors are doing. Study their websites, Google them to see where else they are mentioned. Is there something you are missing out on?

▶▶ Spend a day and an evening hanging out where your customers hang out. What are they interested in? What are they talking about? What are the new things that are exciting them?

▶▶ Pay a visit to your suppliers and find out as much as you can about how they operate. Decide whether they will be able to jump fast and provide the back-up you need if you spot an opportunity you want to seize.

CHAPTER 17

BREAK THE RULES

When Canadian journalist Scott Abbott and his photo editor friend Chris Haney invented the board game Trivial Pursuit they started out by having to sell each game at a $60 loss.

They managed to produce a prototype batch of 1,100 games with some financial support from friends but the numbers did not come close to stacking up. Each game cost them $75 to manufacture, an unthinkable amount for a board game, and they sold it to retailers for $15 so the retailers could sell it on to customers for $29.95 – itself still considered an exorbitant amount at the time to pay for a board game.

Even when they increased production to 20,000 units for their second production run they realised they were so in debt that even if they managed to sell all 20,000 they would still barely break even. Worse still, few people had any interest in buying the game. Many people would probably, and understandably, have given up at this stage.

But the pair did not give up. They spent three years trudging round sales fairs, shopping malls, and even gave home demonstrations trying to drum up interest in Trivial Pursuit. It was really hard work trying to persuade anyone to stock it, and even harder work trying to find someone willing to distribute their game for them.

It was not the most sensible or obvious way to start a business. The first and most basic rule of enterprise is, after all, that you must sell your product for more than it costs you to make in order to generate a profit. But, incredibly, it eventually worked. In 1982 Scott and Chris finally managed to get a distributor to take on their game. The more games they produced, the lower the unit cost of production fell until they were eventually able to make a profit on each game. Within two years it was a massive hit, selling twenty million units in 1984 alone. Trivial Pursuit has now sold more than eighty-five million units around the world and in 2008 games company Hasbro, which had been making the game under licence, paid US$80 million for the rights to Trivial Pursuit, making its two creators very rich indeed.

Channel Frank Sinatra

One of the most compelling reasons for starting a business is knowing that this is the one area in life where you really can do it your way. There are few areas in life where you can genuinely tread on untouched snow but amazingly, thrillingly, starting up a business is one of them. No, it makes no sense to sell a product at a huge loss. But some-

phenomenon that it was the one people always mentioned as being the exception to the rule. But Judy decided to ignore all the naysayers and plough ahead regardless. In the end it took her ten years to get the project off the ground and along the way she had to sell her flat to fund the costs she was incurring, even before she had managed to get formal permission from Björn Ulvaeus and Benny Andersson, the members of ABBA who had written the songs, to let her use them.

But she persisted. And just look at her now. Her musical *Mamma Mia!* opened in London's West End in 1999 and the show was an instant success, selling out every night for weeks in advance. And that was just the start. *Mamma Mia!* has since grossed over £1 billion at the box office, has opened in 160 major cities round the world and has been seen by over thirty million people worldwide. Then in 2008 *Mamma Mia!* was made into a film staring Meryl Streep and Pierce Brosnan.

The film version has become one of the highest-ever grossing films in the UK and together the success of the musical and the film have made Judy Craymer one of the richest women in the country with a personal fortune of £80 million. Yes, the numbers are utterly staggering.

That is what can happen when you decide to break the rules.

Don't be afraid to question the way things are done

a rather more prosaic level, you can go a long way simply asking questions that you are not supposed to ask. Charlie

times someone will succeed doing just that, and by doing a hundred other things that are, on the face of it, wrong and foolish, too. Rules are not there to be blindly followed; they are there to guide and to suggest – and then possibly to completely ignore. You are not at school any more. You really can do whatever you want. And that is what makes entrepreneurship so very exciting.

When Victoria Barnsley started up her publishing company Fourth Estate at the age of twenty-nine she freely admits she had absolutely no idea what she was doing. She says her father would beg her to give it up and get a proper job for fear that she would lose lots of money and be the ruin of the family. In fact, even the name Fourth Estate reflects how little she knew about the industry – Fourth Estate is a term used to describe journalists and the media and she chose it because she planned to publish non-fiction books written by journalists. Within a couple of years, however, she realised that it was impossible to run a solid business based on publishing those kinds of books because their subject matter and popularity was totally unpredictable and the books needed to be published very speedily so they weren't out of date by the time they hit the bookshops.

However, Victoria soon found that the big advantage to being a newcomer to the industry was that it meant she was free to do things her own way. So she did.

When she produced a book with a white cover everyone told her she couldn't do that because no one ever bought books with white covers. But she ignored them and published it – and it was such a success that soon everyone else started publishing books with white covers, too. Then she took another risk by deciding to keep the paperback rights to Fourth Estate books rather than selling them on, as publishers traditionally did. That worked a treat, too.

As Victoria herself says: 'To start with we broke the rules because we didn't know the rules. Then we got a bit cheeky and realised we enjoyed breaking the rules. I learnt that there is no one way of doing things.'

In fact, one of her biggest successes came about as a direct result of breaking the rules, when she decided to publish an unlikely little book called *Longitude* by Dava Sobel. It had already been turned down by dozens of well-established publishers because conventional wisdom in the industry was that no one would ever buy a book on such an obscure scientific subject – and at that time they were unlikely to buy a book that was far shorter than the average book. Victoria decided to publish it regardless. It shot straight to number one on the bestseller list and has since sold hundreds of thousands of copies. A four-part television series based on the book was even made, starring Michael Gambon and Jeremy Irons.

Let's see what happens if . . .

Never let anyone tell you that something can't be done. And never catch yourself saying it to anyone else, either. The most important questions that an entrepreneur can ask are: Why? Why not? Why is it done this way? Why not this way? And then, of course, followed by the most important sentence which begins, Let's see what happens if . . . This is the most exciting thing about starting a business and this is why it is

always going to be the most brilliantly exciting exper no matter what happens.

The secret is to approach everything with a completely mind, read as widely as you can and listen to as many p as you can. And then make your own mind up about th

Jane Packer, the founder of Jane Packer Flowers, has brilliantly out of breaking the rules. When she opened first flower shop, a flower arrangement meant cultiv carnations and chrysanthemums stuck in lumps of oasi traditional designs. But Packer had a clear vision in her h about how she wanted her flowers to look. So she bann carnations and chrysanthemums from her shop and ev weekend would drive out to the countryside and pick wi flowers from meadows to put in her shop instead.

It was a bold move in an industry which had remain unchanged for decades and everyone thought she completely crazy. But it worked. Jane's individual style quickly noticed by magazine stylists who started mak beeline for her shop in search of inspiration and Ja commissioned to write a book on floristry. She now h shops around the world and runs her own floristry Turnover for the combined venture is £7 million

Judy Craymer has broken the rules even more larly. When she decided to write a musical ba songs of ABBA everyone thought she was dou firstly because at the time ABBA's music unfashionable and something people would liking, and secondly because everyone knew ever made money out of writing musicals. tion to that had been *Cats*, and its success

Bigham set up a company called Bighams making fresh food meal kits which customers could cook themselves very quickly at home. He was renting a small catering unit in west London and was doing quite well supplying his meal kits to Waitrose. But one day Waitrose told Charlie that, while they liked what he was doing, his little catering unit was not really a good enough place to make food they sold in their supermarkets because it didn't meet all their stringent health and safety standards. And so, if he wanted to continue to supply them, he would have to move to much larger premises. Charlie told them he would be delighted to, but that to be able to finance the move he would need to start making more profits. And that meant he would need to get more orders from Waitrose. His plain speaking worked. The following week Waitrose tripled his order and Bighams suddenly went from supplying four different recipes to fifty Waitrose shops to supplying twelve different dishes to seventy shops. As a result, Charlie was able to move into a building five times the size of his catering unit and Bighams now has a turnover of £7.5 million a year.

Mark Ellingham, founder of the Rough Guide travel books, also used a similar tactic. When the company which distributed his books went bust, thousands of Rough Guides which had already been printed were left sitting in a warehouse. Mark desperately wanted to buy them back to stop them falling into someone else's hands, but he didn't have the money. So he asked Penguin if they would like to become his new distributor – and also lend him enough money to buy the unsold stock. It was a highly unusual request, but it worked. Penguin gave him an interest-free loan of

£400,000 and Mark was able to buy the books. As he puts it: 'If you don't know how deals are supposed to work then you can just suggest exactly how you want them to work.'

Business plus children can work too

Anna Gibson and Philippa Gogarty also decided to rewrite the rulebook, and with great success. As full-time mothers with six young children between them, and absolutely no experience of running a business, they were not the most obvious candidates to become the UK distributors of the micro scooter, a three-wheeled scooter for children. Especially because they had no intention of putting their children in childcare or leaving them with nannies while they went to work five days a week in an office elsewhere. Instead, they found ways of working in the small pockets of time squeezed in around looking after their children, and they discovered that it was just about possible to make business phone calls with a cacophony of children in the background. And somehow they made it work.

Anna says: 'We would work for three hours in the morning when the youngest ones were at nursery and then we would work until two in the morning once the children had gone to bed. We were always there at the school gate to pick them up. I remember talking to a shipping agent when we were in Philippa's kitchen trying to give Marmite sandwiches to six children at the same time as trying to find out how much it cost to ship a pallet from Germany.'

Despite the seeming impossibility of managing to be around for their children and build a serious business at the same time, they have managed it brilliantly, and the company now has a turnover of £4.3 million.

Give something back

Another way to spectacularly break the rules is to turn the very notion of running a business on its head. Once upon a time business was business and doing good was something else altogether. Well, not any more. These days a growing number of far-thinking entrepreneurs are showing and proving that it is possible to start up and run a successful enterprise that does not have making profits as its sole aim. They can improve people's lives at the same time. What's more, social enterprises, as they are known, are no longer pushed to the edges of the commercial world; they are right there in the heart of it. In fact, there are now more than 55,000 social enterprises in the UK, and the number is growing.

Take Kresse Wesling and James Henrit, who make handbags, belts and wallets out of old fire hoses thrown out by British fire brigades. Previously the decommissioned fire hoses would have been dumped in landfill sites but now Kresse and James take them and turn them into beautiful accessories, selling them via their website. Then they donate 50 per cent of their profits to the Fire Fighters Charity.

The idea for the venture was dreamed up when Kresse spotted an old red fire hose and dragged it home to show James to see if he could do anything with it. The linings for the bags and wallets are all made from recycled materials, too, such as textiles from old office furniture, scrap sailcloth and waste parachute silk. The two of them also make shopping bags for Sainsbury's from old coffee sacks, which would otherwise have been thrown away.

Kresse says: 'We are firm believers that you are not going to save the planet with a doom and gloom message. You are going to save it by making it fun and exciting and engaging for everybody.'

Justin Francis is founder of Responsible Travel, a website that deals with travel companies which are of benefit to people and the environment. He believes there is no need to choose between being profitable and having good values.

'A business should be able to hold together more than one thought,' he says. 'Profit and principles can go hand in hand.' Justin founded the company with £30,000 from private investors in the belief that the travel industry could be changed if people chose holidays that treated communities and the environment with respect. The company's ethos has attracted highly committed staff and clients and Responsible Travel now has an annual turnover of £920,000.

However, Justin realises that being ethical alone is not enough. He maintains the highest possible standards in all aspects of his business so that he can compete in the travel market. He says: 'The business has got to be great; being a social enterprise is not an excuse.'

Glasgow-based firm Haven Products is also managing to combine making profits with pushing for social change. More than 80 per cent of the staff employed by Haven, which provides services for companies that wish to outsource their production processes, are disabled.

However, Managing Director David Whyte is determined

that the company should attract clients because of the quality of its services, not because of the nature of its staff. He says: 'Our focus is on offering clients high-quality, commercially driven services with a great team behind them – who happen to be disabled.'

Around five per cent of each staff member's contracted time with the company is spent learning social and business skills in an on-site learning centre.

Never forget, your business can be anything you want it to be. If you really think you have found a better way of doing things than conventional wisdom would suggest, then do it, and be proud in doing it. Your success will be all the sweeter.

ACTION PLAN

▶▶ Practise breaking the rules in your own life. Do something you would never normally do – do a ocssion of yoga, take a day trip to Paris, go drystone walling, talk to someone on the bus. Liberate your mind.

▶▶ Learn how to say no. Listen to what everyone has to say, but then make up your own mind, no matter how forceful people are. Never forget that it is your business.

▶▶ Practise blocking out the noise of opinion around you and listening to your gut instinct. If you feel really strongly that you want to do something one way and not another, despite what conventional wisdom might suggest, then allow yourself the freedom to try it out in a small way and see what happens.

CHAPTER 18

GIVE IT SOME ATTITUDE

When Ian Wilson started his travel company Wexas he decided that he really wanted to enjoy the experience and not feel that he had to put the rest of his life on hold in order to do so. For him that meant still being able to pursue his other passions in life. So he carefully structured his business in such a way that he could spend four months of every year travelling around the world. He did this by setting up his venture as a membership club in which members pay an annual fee to join and in return receive discounted travel. This limited the number of customers and made administering the bookings much simpler. Then, as soon as the business could afford it, he employed a managing director to run the operation in his absence.

Ian has run the company that way ever since, often taking his wife and two children with him on his trips, which usually involve surfing, diving and sailing in far-flung places such as the Turks and Caicos Islands.

It was a radical step to take, but for Ian it made perfect sense. He says: 'I don't measure success just by size and profitability. I measure success by whether I am feeling fulfilled by what I am doing. I can't see the point of people working every hour they have in order to become the biggest and the best and the richest if it is only to die suddenly of a heart attack having had no time to enjoy it all. I think you should enjoy it while you still have the chance.'

Even better, taking four months off a year does not seem to have unduly harmed his business's prospects either – Wexas now has 25,000 members and annual sales of £40 million.

When you start up a business the secret to success pretty much boils down to something completely intangible: having the right attitude. In a nutshell that means three things:

▶▶ Enjoy it.

▶▶ Have a sense of humour.

▶▶ Have a regular reality check.

Enjoy it

Let's start with the fun bit. I'm not talking about treating the whole thing as if it were a joke and I'm not talking about dissolving into fits of laughter every day, although that may happen at times. I'm talking about the importance of enjoying yourself along the way. Being an entrepreneur is a journey, not a destination. And that is not some wishy-washy new age sentiment; it is actually how you need to approach it. It is, if you like, a state of mind rather than the number of zeros on a cheque. If you are going to have any chance of staying the course, you need to approach it with the kind of attitude that says, right, let's have some fun with this and see where it takes me.

For many people, starting up their business represents a chance to take control of their lives for the very first time and to shape it in the way they choose, instead of being stuck in a rut working for someone else. That is a truly incredible thing to be able to contemplate and it is an amazing opportunity. Only a few generations ago it would have been unthinkable for anyone without access to wealth and privilege. So, think for a moment about the shape you would like your new life running your business to take and make sure you include all the things you think you are going to enjoy most.

Now that doesn't necessarily mean taking such a radical step as Ian Wilson did and disappearing to remote parts of the world for four months every year, but it does mean remembering why you are doing this, and at the very least holding on to your sense of humour when things go wrong. As they inevitably will.

Listen to what people who have been there and done it have to say on the subject. Bill Jordan, who founded Jordan's Original Crunchy after being inspired by tasting honey-baked granola in California back in the seventies, says: 'Have fun. A business is a series of decisions and you have to keep making the right decisions. It usually involves a lot of time and effort and you are not going to do that if you don't enjoy it. So try to ensure that you are doing what you want to do, otherwise it is a waste of time.'

Philip Vecht, founder of Admedia, which puts adverts on the back of toilet doors, says: 'Try to enjoy it on the way up. Even when we were being successful, it was so easy to get caught up in immediate problems and not reflect on what we had achieved and see the bigger picture.'

Frankly, if is not fun and it is not enjoyable, then what on earth are you doing it for? Life is too short and success is too unpredictable to spend all this time and effort starting and growing a business purely in the hope of making a fortune. Yes, the success part happens to some people. But it certainly doesn't happen to everyone and spending many years of your life pursuing a fortune you may never get and hating every minute of it along the way seems a rather pointless way to go.

Have a sense of humour

As well as the desire to enjoy yourself and have fun, the other things you are definitely going to need in your kitbag are a sense of humour when things go wrong, as they in- evitably will, and a sense of perspective to help you realise that perhaps losing that order/investor/warehouse was not actually that important after all. Or, at least, that it was important but that you can survive without it.

Rubbish stuff is going to happen on your way to creating your successful business. It's inevitable. But if you can laugh in the face of adversity, you will win even when you are losing. It is all down to having the right attitude.

When serial entrepreneur Chris Gorman lost £500,000 setting up a recording studio and record label that went bust within a year, his first reaction was relief that he had not done it later in life when he might have lost £20 million. His second was to regard the episode as something to learn from.

He says: 'It was a great learning experience for me to feel the pain of failure because it taught me that I should stick with the things I know and understand.'

Sometimes the disasters can actually lead on to greater and better things. When Alan Black was a teenager studying at technical college he and a friend started up Cavala Electronics to develop new electronic products. One day they built some display panels made from light bulbs and coloured glass that would flash to the rhythm of the music.

They decided to see if any of the big music companies would be interested in buying one, so they made a portable version and drove to London in a van to demonstrate their product. Everywhere they went they met with rejection. 'We went all over the place trying to get people interested in it,' says Alan. 'But it was a total disaster. Everybody said big deal, so what.'

On the way home he and his friend stopped at a café, which had a jukebox in the corner. It got Alan thinking. 'I looked at it and thought that machine would probably be ideal to accept our panels,' he says. The minute he got back to his home in Leeds he looked through the phone directory and found a local firm that sold jukeboxes. The owner asked for a demonstration and was so impressed that he took Alan to a hotel in Bradford to try it on a jukebox the firm had just installed in a disco there.

The owner of the hotel did a deal on the spot for Alan and his friend to install their light panels in all the discotheques in his chain of hotels. Thanks to his optimistic can-do attitude, Alan had managed to seize success from the jaws of defeat and a successful business was born.

Looking back on his life as an entrepreneur, he says: 'I have worked and worked and loved every minute of it. I would work all the time if my wife would let me. It is just natural to me. If I am at home I think I might as well be at work. I am always tinkering about and looking for a new idea or a new invention.'

Adam Pritchard, too, managed to turn disaster into something a lot better. He had decided to try to make pomegranate juice after a friend in India told him he should try it. After learning about its health benefits he thought there could be a market for it in the UK.

So, after several trips to India to meet large producers of the fruit-juice concentrate, he set up a trial to make pomegranate juice. It was a really important moment as Adam had already spent a year going to and from India and had no money left. Unfortunately, the trial was a disaster. He says: 'This pink, gloopy mixture poured out of the machine on to the floor because they didn't know how to process it properly. At that point I thought it was all over.'

But having come this far he was determined not to give in, so he went to the British Library and discovered that the only other country in the world that produced pomegranates in any volume was Iran. Unfortunately it was 2002 and America was preparing to invade neighbouring Iraq, but Adam was not about to let a war get in the way of his ambitions.

He managed to get a visa and met the Managing Director of a factory in Iran.

He says: 'He gave me this juice and I tasted it and it was great. It was exactly what I was looking for. It was like finding the Holy Grail.' As a result of his discovery Adam managed to raise £150,000 of investment to get the venture off the ground and started selling his pomegranate juice. His company Pomegreat now has an annual turnover of more than £12.5 million.

Have a regular reality check

You do, however, also need to be careful not to get so carried away with the buzz of your business that you start believing that nothing can go wrong.

When you spend your days telling everyone how fantastic you are and how brilliant your product is, it can be easy to start believing it, too. This is fine, and even desirable in small doses. Every entrepreneur needs more self-confidence and self-belief than the average person if they are going to have any chance of succeeding. But you also need to keep your feet firmly on the ground.

Trisha Mason discovered this the hard way. Trisha started her own business, VEF, selling houses in France to British people, more than twenty years ago and ran it very success-fully for many years. At one point the company was valued at £9 million and employed thirty-five staff.

But in 2003 she moved the head office to shiny new offices in London's Docklands. And even though she only had thirty-five staff at that point, Trisha decided to take a space big enough for sixty because she planned to launch a new worldwide property business and expected to need more staff to answer the phones. This meant that on top of the costly annual rental for her huge space, she was also committed to paying electricity and phones for sixty people. Even worse than that, having taken the office on a three-year rental deal, at the beginning of 2008 Trisha renewed all the contracts for a locked-in five-year deal. The timing could have not have been worse. Just a few months after that the global credit crisis erupted and demand for her business's services evaporated overnight, as British buyers stopped dreaming of second homes in the sun and started worrying about whether they were going to lose their jobs and how they were going to pay the mortgage on their existing homes.

Within months demand had completely collapsed and Trisha had not only to abandon her plans for her worldwide property business, she also had to reduce her existing staff from thirty-five to just five people. But because she was now locked into a five-year deal for rental, electricity and phones for sixty people, she was still having to pay out around half a million pounds in overheads. She tried to negotiate with the landlord to swap premises for a cheaper, smaller space, but without success, and in February 2009 VEF went into administration.

It was a very sad ending to Trisha's dream, especially as she admits that the business might have survived but for the high annual rental bill.

Trisha will one day bounce back with a new venture, I am sure, and indeed one day the market for French homes will bounce back, but it was a sorry end to a once thriving enterprise.

The bottom line is that if you start to believe you are invincible you are going to run into big trouble.

Believing your own hype can be especially dangerous when you start using it to expand your business into areas where it should not really go. David Sanger, the founder of Rollover hot dogs, discovered this the hard way.

David had started up a successful company selling hot dog machines which inserted the sausage right into the middle of the bread, making it a neat and clean way to eat it, having been inspired by seeing hot dog sellers on the streets of Copenhagen. He sold his hot dog machines to pubs and football clubs and then supplied them with the sausages and bread rolls they needed to make them. It was a nicely thriving business, but it was then that he made his big mistake. Flushed by the success of his hot dog machines, he decided to open some hot dog retail outlets in shopping centres. The first three did quite well so he went on a high-speed opening spree with £750,000 he borrowed from the bank.

He admits: 'I got caught up in it. I opened eighteen outlets in eighteen months. But it was an absolute disaster. There were staff irregularities and theft, and the outlets were losing money. But being an optimist, I kept focusing on the good outlets instead of the outlets that were doing disastrously.'

Fortunately, after eighteen months David finally came to his senses and called a halt to the whole venture. Then he spent the next eighteen months closing the worst outlets and franchising the rest, losing an enormous amount of money in the process.

He says: 'It was a huge learning curve. I learnt that you have to focus on the whole picture, not just on the bit of the picture that you want to see. The failure was not in trying retail, the failure was in doing it too quickly and not stopping and analysing whether it was the right course of action.'

ACTION PLAN

▶▶ Make sure you still have time for fun in
your life and don't neglect the small
things you really enjoy doing. It may be
going for a five-mile run, it may be going
to the cinema, it may be spending half an
hour on Facebook catching up with old
friends. Whatever it is, do it, enjoy it, and
don't feel guilty about spending some
time this way.

▶▶ Surround yourself with inspiring, uplifting
people who share your sense of humour.
Ban negative people from your office.

▶▶ Have lunch on a regular basis with an old
friend unconnected with your business
whose advice and opinions you respect
and who you can rely on to tell you when
you are getting carried away with your
own fabulousness. Old school friends tend
to work best for this as they will cheerfully remind you of some humiliating
incident from your past which puts it all in
perspective.

CHAPTER 19

GET OVER THE BUMP

I don't know if you have ever seen the film *Castaway*, which stars Tom Hanks. It made headlines at the time partly because Hanks was the only person on screen for about 95 per cent of the film and so there was virtually no dialogue because he didn't have anyone to talk to. The film tells the true story of a FedEx employee who is involved in a plane crash and ends up being stranded alone on a desert island. After several months of waiting, he realises that no one is going to rescue him. So after much effort he builds himself a raft and sails out to sea in the hope that a passing ship will see him and pick him up. But every time he thinks he is about to reach open water he hits a huge wave which tosses him back to shore and prevents him from getting any further.

He gets more and more frustrated – and goes a bit crazy for a while, perhaps not surprisingly – until eventually he realises that the only way he is going to be able to get over the wave is if he makes a really big, special, focused effort to overcome it. So Tom gets to work and spends ages building a new raft with a really big sail which he puts up just as he hits the wave – and the sail carries him over the wave and out onto the open ocean. Where he is eventually rescued.

I'm telling you about this film because what happened to Tom Hanks is likely to happen to you. And you are going to have to make the same huge, special effort to overcome it. Not that you are likely to find yourself stranded on a desert island – even though the idea might seem quite appealing sometimes when you find yourself knee-deep in invoices and tax returns. But you are going to find yourself up against a huge hurdle and you are going to need to throw all the resources you have at it to get over it.

That hurdle could well be yourself

I speak to many entrepreneurs and small business owners as part of my job at *The Sunday Times* and I keep hearing the same story over and over again. It is enormously exciting to set up a business from scratch and for the first couple of years you are swept along by a wave of enthusiasm and adrenalin. You don't care that you are working around the clock and you don't care that you never get any sleep and never see your family because you are creating something new and exciting and it is all just a fantastic buzz. Sales figures are going up every week and you dream about how you are going to spend your first million.

But then, one day, suddenly and seemingly for no apparent reason, you and your business hit a bump in the road. At least, it may be a bump but it feels like an enormous mountain to climb. Sales become harder to get and every contract won feels like a huge struggle. Even worse, you are not enjoying it so much any more. It all feels endless and it is hard to see any light at the end of the tunnel.

Bam. It's like hitting a brick wall. It can happen at any time and for the owner of the business it can be hugely frustrating and very scary. You have no idea what has gone wrong but you just can't seem to get the momentum going again, to get over the bump and take your business over the other side and on to the next level.

Even worse, you can't seem to get yourself going again either. Instead of jumping out of bed and racing to your office to try and solve the problem, you find yourself pulling the duvet over your head. Or, even worse, you start spending longer and longer hours hunched over your desk in the office desperately trying to get the magic to come back.

Suddenly it's not so much fun any more and you don't know why and you feel bad about it, but you can't find your way back to the excitement and exhilaration you felt when your adventure was just beginning. You feel weary and over-whelmed by it all and it's not nice. Instead of seeing how far you have come, all you can see is just how much more you have yet to do and how much more hard work that is going to entail. The problem is that at this stage there is no easy way out – your firm does not have a track record to attract outside investors so cash flow is a constant nightmare, it is not yet at the stage where you are able to take more than a basic wage from it, and it is still too small to sell as a going concern.

It happens to everyone

Well, the first thing is to stop beating yourself up about it. It is inevitable that, after the exhaustion and madness that comes with deciding to start a business, of planning and getting everything ready and then eventually launching it, there is going to come a time, maybe a few months later, maybe a few years later, when you wake up one morning and suddenly feel a bit flat and jaded and weary of the everyday grind of actually running your business. It happens when people move house, it happens when they get married, it happens when people have a baby – when, after the initial excitement of the first few months, one day you suddenly realise just how many nappies you are going to have to change and how many carrots you are going to have to purée in the months ahead. So it is not surprising that it also happens when you start a business.

If you find this happening to you, you need to take action. And fast. You are in very dangerous territory because if you, the owner of a business, start to get restless and take your eye off the ball, then pretty soon your business is going to be in big trouble. Businesses need powerful, confident leaders, and businesses that stop growing start shrinking. It is no coincidence that it is around the two-year mark that many start-ups fail. Or, worse, that they are left just to wither and die.

The good news is that, just like Tom Hanks and his raft and that wave, you can get over the hurdle and rediscover the sparkle.

How to get the sparkle back

The first step is to go back to basics. Take yourself away from the office or work environment for a few days and do something that you used to enjoy but now never have time for. Stay in a nice hotel. Spend some time doing fun stuff with your family or partner (as in romantic, not business, partner, unless they happen to be the same person . . . and if so, make sure that work conversation is off the menu). Read a book, watch a film, go fishing. Buy a new duvet and get a good night's sleep. Being sleep-deprived always makes everything seem far worse. And begin to remember why it was you wanted to start a business in the first place. Look back at your list of goals and cross off the ones you have achieved. See how far you have come and be proud of it.

Many years ago, when I was a freelance journalist writing endless articles about tedious financial matters for obscure magazines on my laptop at the kitchen table, I would get to the point every so often where I was so utterly fed up with writing about stock market trading systems or global fund investment strategies or whatever that I couldn't bear to do it for a moment longer. So I would immediately start pitching ideas to editors and if I was lucky I would get myself commissioned to do a travel piece about somewhere exotic. The following week I'd be on a plane flying off to Zanizibar, or Tobago, or Guatemala, or wherever I thought the weather might be nice. It didn't mean I wanted to be a full-time travel writer, but to have a break from the daily routine did wonders for the soul.

The next step is to get everyone else involved in your venture excited about the future, too. This doesn't have to be expensive, or disruptive. Invite your major customers and suppliers round for a glass of wine one evening after work and talk to them about your plans for the business. This is what Austyn Smith, the Managing Director of Austyn James Consulting, a wealth management firm in Beaconsfield, Buckinghamshire, does, and with great success. He invites clients and other local firms to regular wine and cheese parties at his offices, inviting twelve people at a time so that they can have an informal discussion about topics of interest.

He says: 'We decided we wanted to create a local presence and we wondered how to go about it. Everyone else was marketing themselves by direct mail and seminars so we thought, let's be different and do something a bit more enjoyable.'

An unexpected benefit of the evenings is that Austyn and his team have become very much part of the community in Beaconsfield.

Austyn says: 'People are always dropping in to our office to have a chat or they come up to me when I am shopping in Sainsbury's or Waitrose. People ultimately buy from people and they can see that we are not a faceless façade, we are real people with real personalities.'

Indulge in a spot of corporate hospitality, small business-style (that is, without the expense). Take your biggest customer to a football match, or to see a play, and buy them a beer at half-time or a glass of champagne during the interval. Organise a day trip to a local farm so they can bring their kids, and lay on a picnic. Even ordering in pizzas one lunchtime for the people you share an office with can do wonders for morale. Who knows: you may even pick up some work this way.

In fact, anything that brings you closer to your existing customers is going to pay off in spades. You already know that they like you, because they buy things from you. So showing you like them in return can take the relationship to a whole new level.

Be innovative

Your next vital step is to start innovating. Now the idea of innovating and introducing new ideas can make entrepreneurs very nervous because it sounds like it is going to cost a lot of money. But innovation is not about spending a lot of money, it is about starting to think a bit more creatively again about what you are doing.

When Jane Packer started up her first floristry business in London she decided to try to get some orders from the gentlemen's clubs on Pall Mall. But she didn't have enough money to print brochures so she decided simply to send them each a bunch of her flowers instead. They attracted much more attention than a brochure would have done and she ended up getting a lot of orders that way.

You could also join forces with another company which fits well with yours and do some joint crossover marketing. I am not talking about grand mergers or big joint ventures; I am talking about the really simple things you can do with other businesses which have a similar customer base, to your mutual benefit. If you run a shoe shop, for example, perhaps you can do a deal with a local beauty salon so that every customer gets a voucher offering them 25 per cent off the price of a pedicure. Or, if you run a sports equipment shop, how about offering one free entry to the local gym for everyone who spends over £50. The big corporate firms do this sort of thing all the time, but you don't need to be big to benefit from cross-promotion. In fact, once you start thinking about it, the possibilities are endless.

Darren Richards did this to great effect. Darren set up the internet dating service Dating Direct and subsequently sold it for £30 million a few years later. After getting the site successfully up and running on its own, he expanded the business by offering its dating services to the websites of other companies with a similar profile of users, such as Channel 4 and GMTV. It meant that Dating Direct got access to more potential customers while the partner companies got a proven branded dating service without having to set one up themselves from scratch. Simple but incredibly effective. It was not long before Dating Direct became the UK's largest dating service with more than a million members.

Respond differently

Even responding differently to people you come into contact with can reap unexpected rewards. Richard Beggs set up an events management company called Moving Venue. He started off doing small parties and events for clients, but he got his big breakthrough when an insurance agent cold-called him and tried to sell him a policy. Instead of telling him to go away and slamming the phone down, as he might normally have done, Richard decided to see if he could get something out of the connection. He told the agent that he would meet him to discuss insurance policies – on the condition that the agent would introduce Richard to some of his other clients so that he could tell them about the services his events management company provided. As a direct result Richard landed a £30,000 contract to organise a social programme for a group of businessmen in London for a conference. His firm now has an annual turnover of nearly £10 million.

Another good way to put the sparkle back into your business is to take your product or service into a new market. That way you have the comfort of knowing your product or service inside out, and the excitement of being back at square one again, just as you were at your launch party. Richard Beggs did this, too. After he had been running his events management company for a while, he too hit a lull. It was doing fine, but, as he put it, 'There were about a dozen events management companies of a similar size which had been competing with us for years and I decided it was time we elevated ourselves out of the small business scenario and showed our clients we were up for the long haul.'

So Richard looked around for an opportunity and when he heard that Sydney had been chosen as the venue for the 2000 Olympic Games, he realised that there would be a huge demand for conferences and meetings there long before the Games actually took place – and that his company already had all the expertise it needed to provide that. So he set up a small office in Sydney with the help of a former employee who had emigrated to Australia, and, when people started holding conferences and presentations to announce and award the building contracts for the Olympic Games, his company was already on the spot with all the necessary expertise to get the work – which it did. The experience gained over there is also proving useful in the run-up to the 2012 London Olympics.

Prue Leith, the caterer, also did this. She set up her own catering company, Leith's Foods, and then used the goodwill and experience she had built up first to open a restaurant with the same name, Leith's, and then a cookery school. Even though each venture was distinctly different from the others, she believed that all three would appeal to the same kind of customer, which meant she would be able to sell to the same customers three times over. And she was proved right. She eventually sold the lot a few years ago for £14 million.

Sometimes putting life back into your business can even be as simple as adjusting the image of your company to match customers' expectations. And that could be something as straightforward as switching from being a sole trader or partnership to becoming a limited company.

John Gandley originally set up his computer services company Gandlake as a partnership with another person, and even when that partner left he continued to run it as a partnership because there didn't seem any point in changing. But he gradually realised that by remaining a partnership he was being put at a disadvantage to his competitors because the large stock market-listed companies and government departments he supplied didn't really understand the concept of partnerships and so were rather wary of them. Being a partnership also meant that he was less visible in the marketplace than his competitors because, as a partnership, he did not have to file accounts at Companies House – which meant that customers and suppliers were not able to look at the accounts, as they could have done if he was a limited company, and reassure themselves that his business was financially stable. In fact, this aspect was a double whammy for John because his company had actually done much better than its competitors and so its financial stability was a key selling point for him, but by remaining a partnership he was not able to take advantage of it. He has now become a limited company – and the cost of doing the paperwork and getting the lawyers involved was more than covered by tax savings and expansion in the first year.

Create something special to aim for

Here's a great way to inject a bit of magic. Why not give yourself and the people you work with – whether employees or outsourced advisers – a real incentive to reach a certain goal. A few years ago Lara Morgan did this at her firm Pacific Direct, which sold toiletries to hotels, and it produced spectacular results. She promised her staff that if the firm's profits ever reached £1 million, she would take them all on holiday to Barbados. At the time, profits were a fraction of that, at around £200,000. The staff got to work and when profits did indeed hit £1 million two years later, Lara promptly delivered on her promise, taking her twenty-six staff to the Caribbean for an all-expenses-paid week-long holiday. The experience did wonders for morale and team building and Lara sold the company for £20 million in 2008.

The good news is that businesses which have something special about them can – and do – bounce back from all kinds of hurdles and setbacks. Rob Law knows this only too well. Rob had started his own company to make and sell Trunkis, a ride-on plastic suitcase for children which he created as part of a design product while at university. He had had some success persuading a few shops to stock his suitcases but he had also encountered some hurdles, notably a temporary ban on hand luggage following a terrorist incident. He also had to change factories in China when the one making his product went bust, and some of the products coming from the new factories had defective catches, which meant he had to spend one summer fixing and replacing them.

He managed to survive all these setbacks, but then came the biggest nightmare of them all. Deciding he needed some help expanding the business, in 2006 Rob went on *Dragons' Den*. Unfortunately, Rob's pitch went disastrously wrong when one of the Dragons, Theo Paphitis, dramatically pulled a strap off a suitcase to demonstrate how shoddy the product was. Rob was publicly humiliated on national television and walked away empty-handed, thinking he might have blown his chances of ever getting an investor on board and terrified that he might actually have stopped the entire business in its tracks.

But the world is a funny place: after the programme aired on television, Rob received thousands of hugely supportive emails from people around the world.

He says: 'People told me they loved the product, that I shouldn't let the show get me down, and that I should just keep on moving forward. It was such a powerful thing to really pick me up after all the hurdles I had had to overcome and the business just went on and up from there.'

Monthly sales of Trunkis immediately trebled. Department store John Lewis agreed to stock the luggage, an external investor came on board and the business took off in a way that no one, least of all Rob, could ever have imagined.

Rob has since expanded the range of Trunkis to include other designs, including a one-off special in the shape of the Gruffalo, a character from a children's book, and Trunkis are now sold in thirty countries worldwide. In 2009 he also launched a range of compatible travel products for children, including a headrest and a play bag. He is also about to launch a portable booster seat for children which turns into a backpack for easy carrying. All designed by Rob and his team. Turnover is now £5 million a year.

Of course, if you are not sure that your business really does have a future, you need to get in expert assistance in the form of business advisers to help you cast a long, cool eye over the accounts. But if it does have a future, then, whatever you do, don't you dare give up on it. As Winston Churchill once said, if you are going through hell, then keep going. When you are sitting on a beach clutching a large cheque in a few years time you will be very glad you did.

ACTION PLAN

▶▶ Take time away from the business – for a day, half a day, or even an hour walking in the park will help – to remind yourself why you wanted to do this in the first place.

▶▶ Tape yourself answering the phone over a morning – leave the tape running for an hour or so, so that you forget it is there – do you sound cheerful and welcoming or annoyed, curt and abrupt? Do you make any attempt to get some value out of the call for your business, perhaps by exploring mutual ground with the caller?

▶▶ Arrange a social event for your customers and suppliers. Buy a few bottles of wine and get them round to your office, if you have one, or to your local pub if not.

▶▶ Draw up a list of businesses that make products or services that complement yours and then find out as much as you can about them. Are they run by an entrepreneurial owner like yourself? It might be worth picking up the phone to have an informal chat about what joint marketing efforts you can do together.

CHAPTER 20

DO IT LIKE YOU MEAN IT

Some time ago I went to interview chef-turned-entrepreneur Marco Pierre White about his growing business empire, which now encompasses restaurants, cookbooks and television shows. He is as well known for his fiery temper as much as his culinary skills and so it was with some wariness that I met him for a chat over coffee at one of his restaurants in London.

I needn't have worried; he was so enthusiastic about all the things he was doing and planning to do that he talked and talked. Our conversation was only supposed to last about half an hour but once Marco got going there was no stopping him. It was really interesting listening to him and it was extremely endearing how enthusiastic and excited he clearly was about it all. But after about an hour and a half I really had to go so I said goodbye and left to get a taxi. That didn't make any difference. Marco simply followed me out of the restaurant, across the road and down the street, talking all the while and waving his arms in the air to stress the points he was making. He was still talking as the cab drove away with me in it, even though I could no longer hear him.

I can't emphasise enough how important it is that you are passionate about what you are doing when you start up a business. Passion is the single most important ingredient for making a venture work. Without it you are sunk; with it you can conquer the world. Remember, becoming an entrepreneur is not like doing a job; it infuses every part of you and takes over every corner of your life. You have really got to want to do it or it just won't work.

I don't mean that you have to be passionate about staplers or toilet rolls or forklift trucks, or whatever your business is about, as such. Some successful entrepreneurs are indeed genuinely passionate and strongly enthusiastic about the product they are selling, often because it has some emotional link with their childhood. They might have built the business on a recipe handed down from their great-grandmother, for example, or they might be using a skill taught them by their father. Or they might have resurrected an ailing family firm, or created a business in the grounds of the family farm. Angela Wright did just this, building her Crealy Adventure Park for children on her parents' farm in Dorset and getting the whole family involved. It has been a great success; she has since opened another park in Cornwall and the business now has a turnover of more than £6 million.

But many other successful entrepreneurs are passionate purely about the process of building up a great company and making it work, rather than the product itself. For them it doesn't really matter what the product or service they are selling is, as long as it is something they can sell a lot of, and to the best of their ability. That's fine, too. Philip Green might not get too excited about women's clothes as such, but you can bet he gets pretty excited about how quickly they fly off the rails at Top Shop.

Darren Tilley, the founder of specialist chauffeur-driven car business Driven Worldwide, is the perfect example of this. He got to a point in his life where he just really wanted to start up a business and didn't really mind what it was. He says: 'I always had a desire to start something from scratch. I wasn't really that fussed what kind of business it was. For me, it was all about the freedom and variety and the constant challenge that running a business gives you.'

He was, however, passionate about creating a business that actually delivered on its promise to customers. He says: 'You have to feel like you are doing a good job. You have to be passionate about this. As long as I make customers happy it doesn't actually matter what I am selling them.' His approach clearly works, too – his company now has a turnover of £8.5 million.

The bottom line is that it doesn't matter which aspect of your business you are passionate about, as long as you are passionate about making it a success.

Passion schmassion

Now, the word passionate is totally overused and misused these days, so much so that it has become a silly, meaningless, fatuous word. Take a look at comedian David Mitchell's rant on YouTube about how advertisers use it all the time to describe the most unlikely stuff, such as being passionate about sofas. So I am not going to use it any more (well, OK, very sparingly). But whatever you call it, you do need to be very strongly enthusiastic about what you are doing because otherwise you are simply not going to care enough about it to want to make it work.

You are also going to find it a lot harder to persuade other people – whether customers, suppliers or investors – to come on board. Other people will quickly see through you if you aren't fully committed and they will be reluctant to commit, too. Genuine excitement and enthusiasm are infectious and the way you talk about your products or services will straight away take you more than halfway to where you want to be at the end of the conversation.

Anna Gibson and Philippa Gogarty, who have managed to build their £4.3 million business based entirely on their very real passion for the children's micro scooters they sell. They were both full-time mothers but one day Anna was walking in the park with her toddler son Edward when he spotted a three-wheeled micro scooter in the playground and refused to get off it.

'I knew straight away that it was brilliant,' says Anna. 'Edward was ridiculously active and wouldn't sit still for a minute so it was heaven to find something for him that he could do.' When she bought him one of his own she instantly loved the freedom it gave them both. She was constantly being stopped by other mothers asking her where they could buy one too and so Anna started informally distributing micro scooters to mothers living locally, storing them behind the sofa and under beds at home. One day she couldn't get hold of the distributor and so she rang the Swiss head office of Micro Mobility, which made the scooters. The chief executive asked her if she would be interested in becoming the official distributor herself and so she and her friend Philippa flew out to Geneva to meet him and took on the distributorship, despite knowing nothing about running a business. But they far exceeded expectations, selling 30,000 in two years instead of the 8,000 target they had been set, and now they sell 120,000 scooters a year.

Anna puts all their success down to the sheer enthusiasm she and Philippa have for the product they sell.

She says: 'I just knew that it was a fantastic product and that it worked. When we went to see John Lewis department store we were two mums saying, "this is a brilliant product" and they could see that we were passionate about it. The bottom line is that we believe in that scooter. We still get excited when we see children on them.'

Will King's passion for his product has also taken him a long way. Several years ago Will invented a shaving oil for men with sensitive skin and started up a business called King of Shaves to sell it. He has since launched a razor, called the Azor, to go with it, and as a result has already managed to build a business with retail sales of around £80 million. But he does not plan to stop there and his self-declared mission is one day to be bigger than his much larger rivals, Gillette and Wilkinson Sword. Indeed, he is so enthusiastic about his business that he updates his status on Facebook every hour or so, telling the world how well sales are going, or what product he plans to launch next, or what people think of it, or what other people have written about it.

In fact, Will never stops, day or night, enthusiastically updating his progress. Which is lovely and really quite charming, but being his Facebook friend meant that every time I logged on, the first twenty status updates would be from him and sometimes I just wanted to see what my other friends were up to. Which is why I have had to remove him as a friend. Sorry, Will.

Falling in love is easy

Of course, what invariably happens next for many people is that even though they could just as easily have started up one kind of business as another, they find themselves drawn into loving their products or services anyway. That is why you often get successful entrepreneurs claiming to be passionate about the most unlikely things. Many years ago when I was in the sixth form at school I got a Saturday job working in a toy shop. I didn't really have any great interest in children's toys at the time; I was seventeen and had long since grown out of all of that childish stuff and was much more interested in boys and clothes. The only reason I applied for the Saturday job at the toy shop was because I thought it would be a lot less effort than working at McDonald's, which I had done previously. But the inevitable happened. It was the most wonderful Aladdin's Cave of a shop with a whole range of toys, from plastic flies for a penny to Steiff bears selling for hundreds of pounds, and it wasn't long before I was totally immersed in the products stocked in the shop. I remember the huge excitement when new orders came in. We would rip open the boxes and get ridiculously excited about all the new toys that arrived, to the extent that most weeks I would end up buying something out of my pay packet. Even though I clearly wasn't seven years old and had absolutely no use for the furry puppets or teddy bears with surprised expressions that ended up accompanying me home. And I was just the Saturday girl.

It's the same for entrepreneurs. It starts off as a mild interest in a product that you think will sell well, then at some point that changes to being a stronger interest, then suddenly, without you realising, it has become part of your life and something that you can't imagine not doing. Indeed, many entrepreneurs go on to become ambassadors for their products long after they have sold their businesses. Lizzie Vann, who founded Organix, a company which makes organic food for children, for example, has since become a campaigner for better food for children.

Helen and Simon Pattinson are classic examples of how enthusiasm can unexpectedly take hold. They had given up their jobs working for law firms in London and were travelling around the world in search of inspiration for a business they wanted to set up. They had no idea what sort of venture that would be and were looking at anything and everything. In other words, they were clearly not at this stage passionate or excited about selling anything in particular.

Helen says: 'We had a notebook and we would write down anything. We came up with some quite ridiculous ideas.'

When they reached the town of San Carlos de Bariloche

in Argentina, in the foothills of the Andes, they discovered that it was full of wonderful chocolate shops and Helen suddenly realised that there might be a gap in the market in the UK for a chain of shops selling high-quality chocolate. They returned to the UK and, after doing some research into the chocolate market, opened their first shop, Montezuma's, in Brighton. As well as having seven shops the business now sells its chocolate, all of which is made in-house, to two thousand delicatessens and farm shops as well as Waitrose. The company now has an annual turnover of £5 million.

But the really funny thing is that, having started out with a blank sheet of paper and being so open to ideas that they went off travelling around the world in search of them, Helen is now so in love with the products they make that she can't imagine doing anything else. She says now: 'I wouldn't have been able to do this if I had been selling widgets.'

Then add hard work

There is a reason why so many people want to become entrepreneurs and why so few actually take the plunge. It is because it is really, really hard work. You need to have passion and enthusiasm by the sack load, and you need to have a really strong desire to achieve the outcome you want in order to get you through it and out the other side.

While in a café recently I overheard the conversation at the table next to me between two men in their twenties, one of whom was clearly trying to persuade the other to get involved in his business venture. After the first man had done his pitch and talked tantalisingly about the potential of 1,000 per cent or even 1,500 per cent return on investment – 'and that's a lot,' he said helpfully – the other asked simply, 'So what's the catch?' The answer he got was simple and painful – you will have to work really, really hard in order to make it work.

A new business is not a replacement job

If you are starting up a business for the first time because you have been made redundant, I think you need to be particularly careful in analysing your true motivation – and the true level of passion you have for your venture. Although it may be tempting to see starting up a business as a replacement job, with the added bonus that you are now going to be the boss, in reality it is nothing of the sort. Right now there are a great many newly unemployed people falling over themselves in their enthusiasm to start up new ventures, excitedly waving their redundancy cheques of £10,000, or £20,000, and rushing off to PC World to buy a laptop computer and some Excel spreadsheet software. Which is fantastic – but only if you REALLY do want to do it. Ask yourself, would you ever have thought of doing this if you hadn't lost your job? Starting up a business is a risky activity and many start-ups fail within the first three years, so please make quite sure you are doing it for the right reasons. If you have been dreaming about starting up a business for years and being made redundant has finally given you the opportunity, both financially and time-wise, to follow your dream, then that's fantastic. Grab the opportunity while you can and run with it.

But if you start up a business simply because you are fed up with working for someone else, or because there are not many jobs available, or because you quite like the idea of it, or because it sounds like more fun than trawling the jobs pages, then you could be in for a nasty shock. The redundancy money will probably last just long enough to pay for the business cards and the computer and the new website. And then you are on your own, completely and utterly, and all the motivation and drive and investment raised and sales made and profits made will be entirely down to you.

The good news is that provided you have the passion and the enthusiasm to do it, entrepreneurship is a game that can be played by anyone, regardless of age, background, qualifications or anything else. Even better, success really and truly is within everyone's grasp.

A few years ago I started following the progress of three budding entrepreneurs for *The Sunday Times*. The idea was that I would choose three potentially interesting people to follow and would revisit them every six months for three years. It was great fun deciding who to choose – I put a piece in the paper asking anyone interested in getting involved to contact me and received hundreds of replies. One of those I chose to follow was Julie Diem Le, a former eye surgeon who wanted to start up a business creating and selling sunglasses for children because she had seen too often the damage that sun can do to young eyes. She had given up her job and had £30,000 to invest in starting up her first business, which she called Zoobug.

Julie encountered the inevitable hurdles along the way – the terrible British weather which blighted her first two summers in business; the realisation that people in the UK weren't prepared to pay a lot for children's sunglasses so she would have to look overseas for most of her customers; endless design problems when trying to develop sunglasses for babies. She also had to make lots of personal sacrifices, such as moving down to London from Birmingham and having to give up any kind of social life.

But the amazing thing is that, just three years later, Julie had managed to turn that initial investment of £30,000 into a strong, vibrant, fast-growing business which, without any further external investment, now has a turnover of close to £800,000. It is an extraordinary achievement, and she has done it simply by having a good idea and putting it into practice. Julie had never started up a business before but, by taking the plunge, not only has she taken control of her life and her destiny but she has also truly and genuinely, in a small but significant way, added to the sum of human endeavour by protecting children's eyes from the sun.

Now *that* is what being an entrepreneur is all about.

ACTION PLAN

▶▶ Make your passion for your product evident to customers – post a video clip on your website of you talking about your product and why you started up the business.

▶▶ Or make yourself the star of your marketing campaign. Who would remember Remington Shavers if it wasn't for the enthusiasm of Victor Kiam for the product?

▶▶ If you are starting up a business because you have been made redundant then ask yourself, if you were offered your dream job would you prefer to take that than start a business? And what if you were offered it one year into starting your new business? What would you do then?

EPILOGUE

So is it really possible to start a business from scratch and make a million before lunch? Well, it's true that the cheque might not have cleared by the time the food is served, but by using the principles I have laid out in this book it is certainly possible to come up with an idea and a structure for a business in that time which could make you a million – and possibly much, much more.

Creating a business from nothing is one of the most exciting and exhilarating things you can ever do. If you get it right, the rewards can be enormous. And it's not just about the money. Becoming an entrepreneur could open up amazing new opportunities in your life that you never thought possible.

SO WHAT ARE YOU WAITING FOR?

Good luck – and please do let me know how you get on.

Rachel Bridge
rachelbridge.com

APPENDIX

I have had the privilege of meeting a large number of amazing entrepreneurs in the course of writing this book, all of whom have been incredibly generous in sharing their time, their stories and their insights. I've mentioned their businesses by name throughout the book but I thought it would also be useful to list their websites too, so here they are.

At the end I have also included a list of useful organisations for entrepreneurs and small businesses.

ENTREPRENEURIAL BUSINESSES

Admedia
admedia.co.uk

Affleck Property Services
affleckservices.co.uk

A Little Bit of Me Time
alittlebitofmetime.com

Ambition24hours
ambition24hours.co.uk

Applied Language Solutions
appliedlanguage.com

A Quarter Of
aquarterof.co.uk

Architectural Plants
architecturalplants.com

Blink
blinkbrowbar.com

The Book Depository
thebookdepository.com

Emma Bridgewater
emmabridgewater.co.uk

Burts Chips
burtschips.com

Buy Time
buy-time.co.uk

Bybox
bybox.com

The Capital Hotel
capitalhotel.co.uk

The Cheese Shed
thecheeseshed.com

Clinton Cards
clintoncards.co.uk

CocoRose
cocoroselondon.com

Coffee Nation
coffeenation.com

Corrotherm International
corrotherm.co.uk

Crealy Adventure Park
crealy.co.uk

Daily Bread
dailybread.ltd.uk

Danilo Promotions
danilo.com

Dating Direct
datingdirect.com

Digitalstores
digitalstores.co.uk

Dreams
dreams.co.uk

Dress2Kill
dress2kill.com

Driven Worldwide
drivenworldwide.com

Dwell
dwell.co.uk

Elect Club
electclub.co.uk

Ella's Kitchen
ellaskitchen.co.uk

The English Cheesecake Company
englishcheesecake.com

Exposure
exposure.net

The Fabulous Bakin' Boys
bakinboys.co.uk

The Fine Cotton Company
thefinecottoncompany.com

Fire Angel
fireangel.co.uk

Fire Hose
fire-hose.co.uk

Fluxedo Shirts
fluxedoshirts.com

Gear 4
gear4.com

Glasses Direct
glassesdirect.co.uk

Golf Breaks
golfbreaks.com

Haven Products
havenproducts.co.uk

Holiday Taxis
holidaytaxis.com

i-to-i
i-to-i.com

Izzy and Floyd
izzyandfloyd.com

Jonny's Sister
jonnyssister.co.uk

King of Shaves
shave.com

Le Bureau
lebu.co.uk

Liquid Space
liquidspace.co.uk

Mango Mutt
mangomutt.co.uk

Meribel Ski Chalets
meribelskichalets.co.uk

Micro Scooters
micro-scooters.co.uk

Montezuma's
montezumas.co.uk

Moonpig
moonpig.com

Moving Venue
movingvenue.com

MX Publishing
mxpublishing.co.uk

My Warehouse
mywarehouse.me

Not on the High Street
notonthehighstreet.com

Optimax
optimax.co.uk

Ovenu
ovenu.co.uk

Pacific Direct
pacificdirect.co.uk

Pimlico Plumbers
pimlicoplumbers.com

Pomegreat
pomegreat.com

Premier Watercoolers
watercoolers.co.uk

Responsible Travel
responsibletravel.com

Rollover
rollover-uk.com

Rough Guides
roughguides.com

RTG
rtg.co.uk

Streetcar
streetcar.co.uk

Swiss Luggage
swissluggage.com

The Tabernacle
tabernaclelive.co.uk

Tots to Travel
totstotravel.co.uk

Unity group
unity-group.com

VDC Trading
vdctrading.com

Wolseley Wines
wolseleywines.com

Women Speakers
womenspeakers.co.uk

Zoobug
zoobug.co.uk

USEFUL ORGANISATIONS

British Chambers of Commerce
britishchambers.org.uk

British Library
bl.uk

Business Link
businesslink.gov.uk

Enternships
enternships.com

Enterprise Nation
enterprisenation.com

Enterprise UK
enterpriseuk.org

Federation of Small Businesses
fsb.org.uk

Forum of Private Business
fpb.org

Horsesmouth
horsesmouth.co.uk

Intellectual Property Office
ipo.gov.uk

National Federation of Enterprise Agencies
nfea.com

Prince's Trust
princes-trust.org.uk

Shell Livewire
shell-livewire.org

INDEX